Alike and Different:
Exploring Our Humanity with Young Children

Edited by Bonnie Neugebauer

with a foreward by Carol Brunson Phillips

A Beginnings Book for Teachers of Young Children

Published and Distributed by
Exchange Press Inc.
PO Box 2890
Redmond, Washington 98073
(206) 883-9394

Acknowledgments

Sandy Brown — Production Editor
Susan Epeneter — Consulting Editor
Ute Kidder — Customer Service Manager
Dennis Brown — Computer Consultant

Special thanks to Choral Nasser Brown, Diane Burger, Diane Dodge, John Johnston, Ethel McConaghy, Janet Brown McCracken, Katie McGuinness, Karen Miller, Mary Lynn Porter, Maralyn Thomas-Schier, and Francis Wardle.

Photo Credits

Cover, Chapter Two, Chapter Six — Bonnie Neugebauer
Chapter One — Roger Neugebauer
Chapter Three — Subjects and Predicates
Chapter Four — Toni Liebman
Chapter Five — Mary Harrison

Masculine and feminine pronoun references in this book are used randomly for simplicity and in no way reflect stereotyped concepts of children or adults.

ISBN 0-942702-03-4
Printed in the United States of America

Table of Contents

Chapter Three: Staffing with Diversity

Chapter Four: Learning from Parents

Chapter Five: Living in a Changing World

Chapter Six: Considering Our Resources

Foreward

by Carol Brunson Phillips

The content of the education and socialization of young children is always a product of its time—changing as the context in which it occurs changes. For most children, it becomes a special admixture of what the adults in their lives intend for them to learn both for now and for their future, along with what may unintentionally creep into their daily life experiences.

Right now, we know we are raising children to interact in a much different and larger social universe than ours today—in a global economy and in a world community. Alongside this realization we also know that they must learn something different from what we have learned, and that they are, right now, participating in both the intentional and unintentional experiences that will shape their chances to have meaningful and productive lives.

Regardless of what we once may have thought, children do notice differences in people. Very early in life they learn that some differences make a difference and others don't matter, that some are most important and others less so. And as they attach meaning to those differences, they go about forming the intricate maze of knowledge and values, the development of which we still know so little about.

Yet we do know that in this world where children exist, negative values are attached to some human differences; and although we sometimes underestimate the power of children to perceive the unspoken messages in their world, they will in fact come to learn them.

It has been said that actions more often than not speak louder than words. And if this is so in the case of childrearing, then we must be especially vigilant in our actions to shape the values children will attach as they learn about the people in their world. If we don't, they will learn by default the messages that are already prevalent out there in the world, and both we and they will contribute to perpetuating past ideas which we do not want to replicate for our children's future.

I have had the privilege of working for many years in a college of human development, preparing teachers and human service professionals for work with children and families. In doing so, I, along with my colleagues, have discovered that true teaching and learning involves a powerful transformation process which creates new ideas from old ones and uncovers new relations in oneself and in the world. This process gives power and responsibility to each of us to be deliberate in making value judgments about human worth.

An early childhood educator, Carol Brunson Phillips has for 18 years been involved in writing, research, and teacher education—specializing in cultural influences on development. Currently, she is executive director of the Council for Early Childhood Professional Recognition in Washington, DC.

Chapter One
Beginning

"All people, all children, have a common sameness that makes them part of the human race, the brotherhood of man. Sameness and difference should not be seen as opposites; they go together." Francis Wardle, Adams County Headstart, Denver, Colorado

"It Isn't Fair!" Anti-Bias Curriculum for Young Children

by Louise Derman-Sparks

One morning in April, Jean arrives at the child care center clutching a stereotypic Indian warrior in her hand. Another child says to her, "Don't let Suzanne see that. It will hurt her feelings." (Suzanne, one of the staff, is Cherokee Cree.)

Donald, playing at home with his Lego set, turns to his mom and declares, "You know, Mom, all of the Lego people in this set are white people. Why?"

Four and five year olds at Pacific Oaks are beginning to identify, think critically, and care about the ways societal bias affects their daily lives. But why should young children be saddled with such issues, you may ask? Why do they need anti-bias curriculum?

We know that by two, children begin to construct their gender and racial identity and their physical self-concept. We also know (Honig, 1983; Katz, 1982) that, again as early as two, the stereotypes, prejudices, and discriminatory practices pervasive in our society negatively influence this process. Our children grow up in a psychologically, as well as a physically, polluted environment. Their developing attitudes towards themselves and others reflect the poisoning effects. They exhibit pre-prejudice— erroneous beliefs and fears which either mirror adult bias or which, although based on how young children think, may lead to prejudice unless adults intervene.

What are young children thinking and doing?

Steven is busy being a whale on the climbing structure in the two year old yard. Susie tries to join him. "Girls can't do that," he shouts. Steven may want to play by himself, or he may not want to play with Susie. Whatever the reason, he already has gender-based words for rejection in his repertoire.

Robby, three years old, refuses to hold a Black classmate's hand. He says "Yucky" when seeing pictures of Black children in books. At home, he insists, after bathing, that his black hair is now white because it is clean. His mother worriedly relates the incident to his teacher, wondering if he is already prejudiced. The teacher is also concerned. They plan activities to help Robby overcome feelings which can crystalize into full blown prejudice.

Mark picks up a big block. "You're strong," Julie admiringly tells him. "You're strong, too," responds Mark. "No, I'm not," replies Julie. At four, Julie never chooses large motor activity, already confining herself to small motor, quiet choices. Research tells us that by four children monitor each other's behavior.

"Ann can't play with us. She's a baby," Sandy tells the teacher. Ann, four and a half, is confined to a wheelchair. Although walking is a signpost of movement from babyhood to childhood, it is also true that one major form of handicappism in our society is the infantilization of disabled people. Thus, the preschool child's understandable comment is also another example of pre-prejudice.

"You aren't an Indian," another four year old tells Suzanne. "Indians don't live anymore." We have found that preschool children already hold a number of erroneous and negative ideas about Native Americans. This may be the first bias young children learn in our society.

What is anti-bias curriculum about?

Anti-bias curriculum recognizes and provides tools for dealing with the issues raised by these anecdotes (which are only a few of the many we have collected). Grounded in traditional preschool goals and methodology, anti-bias curriculum enables children to comfortably explore the differences and similarities that make up our individual and group identities, *and* to develop skills for identifying and countering the hurtful impact of bias on themselves and their peers. It goes beyond our earlier approach to curriculum at Pacific Oaks, which was focused on activities about people's similarities, but did not directly address differences or *pre-prejudice.*

Pacific Oaks teachers state our goals in the following ways: "I want children to become tolerant, understanding, and compassionate by the time they are five. They need that as a base for the rest of their lives. We're providing emotional nutrition," Molly Scudder (kindergarten) asserts. Mae Varon (preschool) adds, "I want children to learn to discriminate, to make judgments about what's fair and what's not, to sort out what they have the power to change and what they can't do anything

Photograph by Nancy P. Alexander

about." Maria Gutierrez (two year olds) continues, "We want children to become effective thinkers and problem solvers, not accepters of dogma; actors, rather than passive victims." "Children have the capacity for experiencing hurt and despair, and for empathy and fairness. What we are doing empowers them by increasing their understanding and teaching them ways of handling stress. That's more realistic than trying to protect them from knowledge of the world," concludes Cory Gann (preschool).

Anti-bias curriculum is at once a methodology and a particular belief system which values diversity among people—and peaceful, just, and equitable cooperation. We found it was not so much new methods that we needed, but rather thinking about activities from a new perspective and using already existing methods for new issues.

What are the sources of the curriculum?

Daily curriculum emerges from three sources: 1) children's behavior, 2) teachers' awareness of children's developmental needs and learning styles, and 3) societal events. Sometimes the child's comment or behavior is the starting place: *A group of children are playing in the sandbox; the girls cook and the boys dig tunnels. One boy calls out to the girls, "We're finished working now. Get us our supper."* At group time, their teacher decides to read one book about the different kinds of work women do and another book about men doing household work. The next day she helps each child make a book about what kinds of work, at home and out of the home, their own family members do, pointing out the diversity of roles.

Sometimes the teacher introduces an issue: Knowing young children notice and express curiosity about skin color, the teacher of the three's plans a series of activities about this aspect of identity. She has them put their arms out in a circle and talk about each other's skin colors; look at themselves in a full length mirror and talk about their own color; find the crayon and paint which most closely matches their skin, and draw a picture of themselves with it; and use beige, brown, and black, as well as white drawing paper. She reads the book **Colors All Around Us** by Vivian Church (Chicago: Afro-American Publishing Co., 1971), which illustrates the different skin tones of Afro-American children and is also a good starting place for other children, takes color photos of each child and staff member, and makes a poster of all the different skin colors in the classroom.

Sometimes an event in the child's larger community precipitates an activity: Thanksgiving is a case in point. In the weeks preceding this national holiday, children are inundated with stereotypic images and messages about Native Americans. It is impossible to escape the television specials, greeting cards, store decorations, and children's books with one-sided versions of the Thanksgiving story.

Anti-bias curriculum challenges such bias and the already erroneous beliefs and fears preschoolers hold about Native Americans. Thus, we suggest: 1) Introducing four and five year olds to the real, daily life of contemporary Native Americans through photographs, filmstrips, visitors, accurate books. 2) Critiquing stereotypic images in greeting cards, decorations, and books as unfair and untrue by comparing them to accurate images. 3) Having discussions which allow children to talk about their fears and misconceptions (perhaps by using a story as a catalyst). 4) Not permitting the playing of *Cowboys and Indians*, explaining that such games are hurtful to real Native American children. (We might tell a story about one of our Native American doll's negative experiences with other children playing *Cowboys and Indians* as a catalyst for discussion.)

What are anti-bias activities?

Activities fall into three categories, which build on each other. Here are some we have found useful:

• **Exploring physical differences and similarities**

Read **What is a Girl? What is a Boy?** by Stephanie Waxman (Culver City: Peace Press, 1976), which helps children understand that their gender identity is determined by their body parts—not by the clothes they wear, the things they like to do, or how they show emotions.

Activities for learning about skin color are described above. Children also need help understanding: 1) that skin color comes from their parents and 2) that there is a range of skin color within each family. Collect or take color photos of the family members of each child. Make a book about everyone's family.

Young children are curious and sometimes fearful about disabilities. They need opportunities to interact with disabled children, to explore the tools disabled children use, and to learn about how to enable disabled children to be as independent as possible. Have crutches, wheelchair, hearing aid, Braille, sign language available for children to learn about and use. Purchase or make a few dolls with specific disabilities. Tell stories, for example, about the doll in a wheelchair going to her preschool the first day and not having any way to get up the stairs. Ask the children what could happen so that the child could get in and out of the classroom by herself.

• **Exploring cultural differences and similarities**

Gender roles—Preschool children's play choices are already strongly influenced by gender norms. Observe children's free play, and help them experience activities and materials they normally do not use. Sometimes environmental changes help (e.g. moving housekeeping equipment— stove, sink, etc.—to the block area encourages crossover and joint use). Sometimes more direct intervention is necessary (e.g. a *girl's day* each week in the block area, until they are comfortable using the blocks on their own). Modeling, visitors, books, pictures, and stories provide children with data about the many different behaviors and jobs carried out by women and men. Consciously include roles which contradict prevailing stereotypes.

Ethnicity—This aspect of anti-bias education, under the name of multi- cultural curriculum, exists in many early childhood programs. Unfor- tunately, the methodology often reinforces rather than challenges stereo- typing. Activities tend to center on holiday celebrations, and on objects and food, taken out of context of people's daily lives. This is *tourist* curriculum. Children *visit* a culture for a day, or maybe a little longer (if they are doing a unit) and then go *home* to a classroom which does not integrate different cultures into its own daily life. Moreover, by focusing on holidays, we give children the impression that other people spend their time in ceremony, instead of going to work, raising children, living.

Preschool children are developmentally ready to explore cultural differences in the context of each of their family's life. This means learning, for example, about how Sam's family, who are Japanese Americans, live their daily lives—who is in their family, what roles they play, what work they do, what objects they use in their daily life, what food they eat regularly, as well as what holidays they celebrate. Sam's classroom should include: written signs and tapes in Japanese, artifacts used in his home in the dramatic play area, Asian dolls, books about Japanese American children, and authentic pictures and wall posters depicting contemporary life of Japanese Americans in the United States.

By basing ethnic cultural activities in the life of each child's family, we avoid the dangers of stereotyping a group by implying, for example, that all Japanese Americans live the same way. We avoid a *tourist* approach by placing cultural behaviors in context, and by incorporating aspects of each child's way of life into the classroom.

Find out from each family how they practice their ethnic heritage at home. Invite parents to school to tell stories about their family members, their history, to show objects, cook foods, celebrate a holiday. Make books about each family's way of life; have a wall display of *Our Families*, with photos of extended family members doing a variety of jobs in and out of the home; have books about different kinds of families. Learning about each child's family generates curriculum for a whole school year. If your class is ethnically homogeneous, begin with the differences among families in your class, and then branch out, still keeping to the approach of individual families.

Photograph by Subjects and Predicates

• **Learning to challenge stereotyping and discriminatory behavior**

Developing skills for challenging unfair behavior begins with one-on-one interactions between children. We already invest considerable time in helping them develop assertiveness and nonviolent conflict resolution skills. Anti-bias curriculum extends these skills to discriminatory situations.

Role model non-acceptance of such behavior. Regardless of what you think may be the underlying reason, do not ever permit a child to reject another child because of gender, race, ethnicity, disability, or to use derogatory terms about another child's identity. We consider such behavior equivalent to hitting or throwing a heavy object at another child, and we deal with it as we deal with physical aggression. We stop the behavior first, comfort the child who has been the target, and then find out from both what was going on and take action accordingly.

Develop critical thinking about stereotyping in books, television, and toys. Compare and contrast accurate photos and illustrations with inaccurate and stereotypic images. Explain how untrue pictures are unfair and hurtful because they make fun of people.

Involve children in group action. For example, Bill Spark's mainstreamed, public school classroom faces the handicapped parking spaces. He noticed that a few teachers were not honoring the spaces. The children went to look at the parking spaces, talked about the handicap sign, and why these places are reserved.

Following a discussion of what to do, the children decided to make parking tickets to put on the cars of non-disabled teachers parked in the handicap zone. After a week of this activity, the spaces were left free for people who really needed them.

Another group action, this at Pacific Oaks, dealt with a frequently used object in children's lives. Lissa, a child care center teacher, decided one day to do something with the children about *flesh colored* bandaids. She explained that the box said the bandaids matched people's skin color, and suggested they find out if this was true. Each child put a bandaid on and determined whether or not it matched their skin color. They made a chart of their results.

They then decided to have children from other classes also test the *flesh colored* claim. Finally, they dictated and mailed a letter to the manufacturer. Eventually, they received a letter, with coupons for transparent bandaids! Although this activity was not sufficient to get the company to remove the *flesh colored* claims from their boxes, it did teach the children about taking action when they think something is unfair.

How do you get started?

• Do some background reading (see "Resources on Diversity" in this book).

• Form a support group with whom to study, plan, evaluate throughout the year. This group can include interested parents and teachers in your school, or teachers from other schools. A support group empowers you to try new, and possibly controversial, activities and to make and learn from your mistakes.

• Begin with an aspect of anti-bias curriculum you feel most comfortable with; judge what will work best in your setting.

• Plan how to involve parents (and administrators) from the beginning, informing and including them in developing activities.

We found developing anti-bias curriculum is always stimulating, at times exhilarating, at times painful. It has meant finding more effective means to put into practice our basic commitment to children.

For information about the curriculum guide upon which this article is based, write to:

Louise Derman-Sparks
Pacific Oaks College
#5 Westmoreland Place
Pasadena, CA 91103

References

Honig, Alice. "Sex Role Socialization in Early Childhood," **Young Children**, September 1983, 57-70.

Katz, Phyllis. "Development of Children's Racial Awareness and Intergroup Attitudes," in Lilian Katz (ed.), **Current Topics in Early Childhood Education**, Vol. IV, Urbana, IL, 1982.

Louise Derman-Sparks is a member of the faculty at Pacific Oaks in Pasadena, California. She has also taught preschool and directed a child care center. She is interested in developmental theory and how child and adult viewpoints are influenced by the socio-political contexts within which they live, particularly in the area of racial/ethnic identity and attitudes.

Talking About Differences Kids Notice

by Elizabeth Crary

You and a group of preschoolers have just left the pet store. Carvis sees a tiny man and asks loudly, "Why is he so little? Did someone chop his legs off?"

Teresa and Gina are playing with the blocks. Teresa's aunt Alice comes to pick her up. When Alice bends over to help pick up the toys, Gina notices her withered hand and red skin from a birthmark. She asks in a curious voice, "Why is your hand so funny?"

Preschool children have a natural curiosity that helps them gather information about their world. In general, teachers and parents encourage this interest by responding promptly to their questions. However, there are times when children's questions embarrass adults who don't know how to respond. Questions about physical, ethnic, or racial differences are difficult questions for many people. When you respond abruptly or ignore the questions, most children conclude something is wrong with them or with the other person.

Children also gather information by watching how adults respond to these people. If we are uncomfortable or ignore them, children often conclude there is something wrong with the person. Following are ten guidelines for dealing with these awkward questions and for becoming more comfortable with different kinds of people.

• **Respond promptly.** If possible, answer the child's questions immediately. If it is not possible, tell the child when you will answer. Then, when the time comes, bring the subject up and answer the questions. Sometimes people are tempted to let the subject drift if the child forgets. That, however, gives children the message that the topic is too difficult or uncomfortable to deal with.

ve simple answers. According to Piaget, young children need simple vers which relate to their experiences and observations. "Why is that n so dark (or light)?" can be answered in terms of families rather than ace. "He is dark because his mother or father is dark. You have blond hair and light skin just like your mother." Similarly, "Why is that man so little?" can be answered in terms of family rather than genetics. Pre-school children have difficulty understanding abstract concepts—race and genetics are beyond them.

• **Model respectful behavior both verbally and nonverbally.** Smile and make brief eye contact as you would with any other pleasant stranger. Many people were taught as children not to stare. They were taught so well that they avoid looking at people with disabilities at all. One severely disabled man commented, "Sometimes I feel invisible. No one will look at me. I wonder what would happen if I fell down or fainted? Would people help me or step over me without seeing me?"

Respond to people with disabilities as you would to other people in the same group. Avoid acting as though they are mentally incompetent just because they are in a wheelchair. Let them answer their own questions rather than answering for them.

• **Respect a disabled person's body space.** Don't lean or hang on to a person or her wheelchair. Don't let children borrow crutches or walkers without getting permission first. In addition, resist the temptation to pat or touch disabled people in ways you would not touch others.

• **Acknowledge children's fears.** Some children are reluctant to approach or discuss people who are different from themselves. This often stems from a fear of the unknown or misconceptions about different people. Many children are suspicious of unusual people—like clowns or Santa Claus—as well as people with physical disabilities. These children resist the new and different. *Slow-to-warm* children need to be encouraged to feel comfortable with unusual people gradually.

Fears of disabled people are best treated as other fears: acknowledge them and offer children tools to deal with their fear. It is rarely effective to tell a child that there is nothing to be afraid of. If feeling comfortable were that simple, no child would be afraid. If you pressure a child, he has two problems—his fear and your disapproval. One helpful way to respond is to reflect the child's feelings, "You are scared of the man without legs," and then give the child tools and experiences to deal with the fear.

• **Clarify misconceptions.** Children are often afraid of disabled people due to misconceptions. Many children think that bad things happen to you when you do bad things. (This idea is reinforced when children are

punished for bad behavior.) In their eyes, someone with a visible
disability must have been very bad. Another common misconception is
that the deformity is contagious. The best way to respond is to clarify
their misconceptions.

When a child has concerns, give correct information. "Simin has had
cerebral palsy since she was a baby. She walks the way she does because
it is the only way she can walk. It is not a sickness you can catch. The
tiny part of her brain that tells her legs how to move does not work right.
All the rest of Simin works fine and will continue to work fine."

In another case, a polio victim with a withered hand, you could say,
"Mark had polio, a sickness, when he was a little boy. The sickness
damaged the part of his brain that makes his hand work. He is well now.
And nobody can get polio from him."

Photograph by Subjects and Predicates

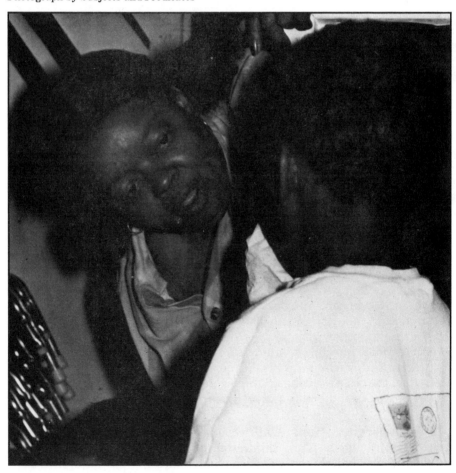

• **Offer help and let the disabled person decide how much help he or she needs.** Disabled people have a need to feel lovable and capable as does everyone else. When people do things for them without asking, they receive a clear message that we think they are not capable of either doing something or of deciding if they need help with it.

For example, if you are at the park and a woman in a wheelchair is having trouble opening the restroom door, you can ask, "Would you like some help?" If she accepts, you could ask two children to hold the door for her.

• **Model patience with people with disabilities.** Give people with disabilities the time they need to be independent. For example, when talking with a man with a speech impediment, give him your undivided attention. Let him finish his sentence rather than finishing it for him. Your *assistance* carries the message that there is something wrong with the way he is talking (unclear or not fast enough). Don't pretend you understand if you don't. It is often helpful to repeat back what he said to clarify what you heard.

• **Introduce differences through books.** For some children it is less threatening to learn about different people first from a book. **Why Does That Man Have Such A Big Nose?** by Mary Beth Quinsey (Seattle, WA: Parenting Press, 1986) illustrates a variety of people (representing ethnic and physical differences) and answers common questions children have in a simple, constructive way. **About Handicaps** by Sara Bonnet Stein (New York: Walker and Company, 1974) helps children feel comfortable with people with disabilities. **Why Am I Different?** by Norma Simons (Niles, IL: Albert Whitman, 1979) discusses differences in abilities and family styles.

• **Offer children experiences with real people.** When children have questions about a *different* person, consider letting them ask that person. Many people with disabilities welcome the chance to educate children. Look at the person. If he appears open and friendly, he may feel comfortable answering questions. You may even know someone who would feel comfortable coming to your center.

Children live in a concrete world and are learning what is real and pretend. Children may want to touch a metal hand, ride in a wheelchair, or touch very wrinkled skin. If children can explore differences openly, they can begin to feel comfortable with all kinds of people.

Some children need to practice or replay what they have seen and learned. They may walk around blind, with crutches, or with uneven gaits. You can explain to these children, "It is okay to pretend to walk like a person with cerebral palsy in school or at home, but not when a person with cerebral palsy is around."

Children notice how the adults and children around them treat differences. It is important for adults to answer children's questions promptly, to verbalize unasked questions, and to model respectful behavior to all people. If the adults are comfortable around people with disabilities, children learn that. If the adults encourage children to talk about differences, children can clarify misconceptions and learn that differences are okay. When children have a chance to meet many kinds of people (different races, ethnic groups, and people with disabilities) they can learn that friendship can accept both the commonness and the difference. You can offer children this gift of friendship by inviting different people to your center and by responding promptly to children's spontaneous questions.

Elizabeth Crary is an author and educator. She is a parent educator at North Seattle Community College; author of several books for parents, teachers, and children; and president of Parenting Press, Inc.

"Where Do We Begin?" Bringing the World into Your Classroom

by Bonnie Neugebauer

The richness and beauty of the world takes many forms—the craftsmanship of a basket, the feel and drape of a sari, the sounds of a lullaby. When we bring bits and pieces of the world into the daily life of our programs, the unfamiliar becomes familiar; what was outside our experience becomes part of our frame of reference. From that point on we have real objects and experiences which serve as a basis for asking questions and initiating conversations.

Classroom Aesthetics

travel posters and magazine photographs which depict a wide variety of places and people (including people of different ages, abilities, life situations); textiles from around the world on the walls and around the room in blankets, cushions, pillows, rugs; drawings by children from other places and with varying ability; distinctive and interesting paintings, sculpture, pottery, baskets, and other arts; mobiles and wind chimes; printed labels in more than one language; a colorful hammock from Costa Rica; containers for storage—pottery, baskets, calabash, lacquered box

Dramatic Play

tea cups; chopsticks; baskets; gourds; kimono; fans; getas; parkas; sarapes; African masks; mukluks; saris; clogs; snowshoes; dashikis; moccasins; beads; beret; turbans; sashes; veils; fans; nets; futons; tatami mats; food containers, recipes, magazines and newspapers printed in other languages; foreign coins; variations of the playhouse (adobe, igloo, tent, mosque, oasis); dolls and puppets—Japanese daruma, Russian Matryoshka stacking dolls, dolls with assorted racial characteristics and handicapped equipment; stuffed animals including camel, iguana, goat, tiger, snake; crutches, braces, heavy glasses, hearing aids, bifocals, canes

Music and Movement

folk songs and recordings for children, translated and in foreign
languages; classical, contemporary, and ethnic music recorded for adults,
in English and in other languages; instruments from other places:
Nigerian talking drums, thumb piano, maracas, bells (when possible,
provide authentic instruments); *white noise*—bossa nova, samba, jazz,
spirituals

Science and Mathematics

manipulatives featuring pictures of foreign objects; raw cotton; cocoa/
coffee beans; chestnuts; lentils; feathers; seeds; plants (bonsai, orchid,
cactus); foreign coins; sketches/photographs of skyscrapers, pyramids,
igloos in block corner (from "Using Learning Centers for Multicultural
Activities" by Elvia Ana Rodriguez and Kent Chrisman, **Texas Child
Care Quarterly,** Fall 1985); figures for block play of varying ages, races,
sexes, physical abilities, and occupations

Language

books that reflect a world view (see "Reflecting Diversity—Books to Read
with Young Children" in this book), books in Braille, books in several
languages, alphabet characters in other languages, wordless books

Taking Up the Slack

In all of this searching for interesting, available materials, there will
undoubtedly come times when you can't find what you want. That's when
you will need to tap your own creative resources and make your own
materials.

—Write a book based on the lives and experiences of the children in your
class. If you can't provide photographs, the children can draw the
illustrations. Fill in with family photographs and magazine pictures.

—Find someone in your program who will make a doll to your
specifications. There are many doll patterns available which will only
need to be modified by fabric, color, and style choices.

—Let imagination fill in some spaces. Describe your vision to the
children and let them adapt it to suit their needs.

—Write your own recipe book, based on the favorites of the families in
your program.

Chapter Two
Meeting the Needs of All Children

"Special needs are normal—everyone has them to varying degrees." Katie McGuinness, Adaptive Environments, Boston, Massachusetts

Obstacle Courses Are for Every Body

by Carol Stock Kranowitz

Two children, as different as chalk from cheese, come to the same classroom every day at St. Columba's Nursery School in Washington, DC. Nathan hurtles in like a cannonball, his treasure-laden backpack bouncing behind him. He is ready for the day, eager to join his friends, happy to converse and sing, nimble and quick in every way. He especially loves make-believe play, donning cowboy chaps or a king's cape, and altering his tone of voice and facial expression to fit the role. He becomes the fearsome wolf, the biggest Billy Goat Gruff, or the mommy in the housekeeping corner with equal delight. Indeed, the only role he refuses to take in dramatic play is that of the baby or the littlest, proclaiming with vehemence, "I'm not a baby; I'm big!"

Nathan must protest frequently about his size because he is a person of short stature. (The preferred term for an individual like Nathan is short-statured rather than a dwarf.) At age four, he is two-thirds as tall as his peers; he will never grow to a normal height. His legs are noticeably short in proportion to his body, causing him to lose his balance when he hops or stands on one foot. Otherwise, his compact body is well-proportioned, and he enjoys more physical prowess than many of his classmates.

Ana is very different. A big little girl, she inches into school with extreme caution, just as she does into play, or conversation, or any new situation. Where Nathan leaps, Ana lingers; where he is outgoing, she is retiring; where he likes to be first, whatever the task or game, she prefers to watch and wait. Her shyness and physical development are normal and age-appropriate for a four year old, yet they impede her initial participation in many preschool activities. Once in the game, however, she is in it wholeheartedly.

Both children have needs, but Nathan's short stature defines him as a child with special needs. As such, he is one among the 10 percent of

Photograph by Gail Lynch

students with special needs who are mainstreamed at St. Columba's Nursery School. Like the other students with differing disabilities, Nathan needs to feel good about his strengths and accomplishments, and to learn problem-solving skills in order to compensate for his difference. He needs to be comfortable with himself and with others who may treat him unfairly, and to mature as a well-equipped, social individual. Indeed, his basic needs are no different from Ana's or from any other preschooler's. All children have needs.

How, then, can a preschool meet the different needs of all its students? The challenge is to find activities that do all things:

• specifically help those children who need a boost in any of the developmental areas—cognitive, physical, social, lingual, or emotional

• build on children's strengths and skills

• sit smack-dab in the mainstream of preschool life, so that they are shared experiences, not private therapy

• appeal to all the children

• remain open-ended in order to explore, not ignore, children's differences

Creating Meaningful Activities for Differing Needs

Arriving at these ideal activities takes some creative thinking. **Begin positively**, with a list of the children's strengths. Helping children to build upon the skills they already have, one small step at a time, is the surest way to achieve a greater goal.

Proceed to **determine the children's primary needs**. Ana's greatest need, for example, is to emerge confidently from her shell. Nathan's is to continue developing his many skills while learning how to function as a short-statured person in a world designed for larger people.

Set realistic goals. For instance, realistic goals are that Ana will feel comfortable about joining in the fun and that Nathan will have many opportunities to prove himself as a capable four year old. Unrealistic goals would be hoping for Ana to become the class boss or for Nathan to adore being mistaken for a toddler.

Next, **brainstorm** with your co-teachers about what **group activities** may be attractive to children with polar needs. All children like to draw to music, allowing the beat of the music to guide their crayons. Creative art work, such as making collages, is appealing. Choosing a song and leading the rhythm band works nicely. Class projects, like cooking or planting a garden, do not require special skills. For Ana and Nathan, an obstacle course is a perfect activity as it encourages them both to develop their large motor skills.

Select an activity, taking into consideration your own abilities and interests. It's easier to provide the children with a meaningful experience if the chosen activity is one you enjoy personally. If you aren't keen on an activity, the children may not relish it either.

Plan and implement the selected activity with regard to the space and equipment available.

After you have presented the activity, **evaluate** how it went. Was it successful? Did the children stick with it? Was it too easy? Too hard?

Refine the activity. Try it again and again until you have a basic formula. When the exercise is worthwhile, the children will always let you know.

If you decide to proceed with an obstacle course, the success of the activity is guaranteed. Every child's body is different, but all bodies share the same need to climb, balance, and stretch. A child with superior athletic skills will enjoy an obstacle course because moving is his specialty. A sedentary child will like it as he learns to maneuver his body in ways he never considered possible—or even desirable. A child with special needs will love it because it is a challenge he can meet in his unique style. In

Problem-Solving Process
(The example used for Nathan and Ana)

1. Ascertain Child's Strengths
Nathan — imaginative, agile, healthy, outgoing, blessed with positive self-image
Ana — persevering, patient, compliant, methodical, aglow with each small success

2. Ascertain Child's Needs
Nathan — to prove he is as competent as, or more competent than, his peers, despite short stature; to improve poor balance due to disproportionately short legs
Ana — to improve large motor skills; to gain confidence in joining groups

3. Set Goals
Nathan — to gain better balance and to be offered the chance to feel tall and big
Ana — to become a bit more adventurous, more sociable, and more comfortable with her body in space

4. Brainstorm: What group activities are suitable?
Nathan — physical activities that require stretching and balancing
Ana — non-competitive experiences that require different kinds of motor-planning and that allow her to proceed at her own pace while participating with her peers

5. Select an Activity (e.g. an outdoor obstacle course)

6. Plan the Activity (see "Planning an Outdoor Obstacle Course")

7. Implement the Activity (see "Building an Obstacle Course")

8. Evaluate the Activity
Nathan — Was he able to stretch sufficiently to climb the rungs and reach across the empty spaces between obstacles? Did he work on his balancing skills?
Ana — Was she willing and able to work through the course? Did she need a teacher's hand throughout? Did she interact with her peers?
Both — Did they do the whole course or did they skip some obstacles? Did they return to a favorite spot? Did they voluntarily repeat the whole course?
All — Did everybody have fun?

9. Refine the Activity—and Try Again!

fact, preschoolers with special needs are so adept at making accommodations for their differences that they can teach their peers new ways of overcoming obstacles.

In theory and in practice, an obstacle course is a foolproof activity. Now all that remains is a little planning.

Planning an Outdoor Obstacle Course

• **Select the site**

An ideal site for an obstacle course is an open, flat, grassy area, removed from swings and ball fields. The site should not be so wide open that children may wander off, or so distant from the storage area that lugging equipment to and fro becomes impractical. Other good sites are a corner of the blacktop playground or a classroom reserved for large motor activities.

• **Plan the course**

The goal of an obstacle course it to awaken the children's kinesthesia, or muscle sense. This is especially important for a child like Ana. The perfect course will engage as many motor skills as possible: balancing, alternating feet, crawling, climbing, somersaulting, scooting, sliding, ascending and descending inclines, leaping, jumping, pulling and reaching, and taking big steps. Mastering each obstacle requires motor-planning. Motor-planning involves eye-foot coordination as well as spatial awareness, an understanding of the relationship of one's body in space.

The simplest course—for the teacher to build and for the children to execute—runs in a great circle. It is linear in design. The first obstacle leads directly to the second, the second to the third, and eventually, the last right back to the first. A logical order of obstacles will help the child understand the sequence and will keep the children moving, one after the other. (Not recommended are courses designed in a straight line, in a figure-eight, or in a radial pattern. In a straight line, children begin and end at a different point and tend to meander away when they have completed the course once. In a figure-eight, the children become confused when their paths cross in the middle. In a radial pattern, with many different obstacles converging at the center, chaos prevails.)

Alternate the obstacles so that the children must vary both their body posture and their form of locomotion as they proceed from one challenge to the next. It is helpful to mutter prepositions to yourself as you work—*up, down, across, through, over, under, into,* and *around.*

Assemble the equipment

3e creative with permanent obstacles on the playground, turning andscape timbers into balance beams and tree stumps into stepping tones. The advantage of using obstacles that are stuck in the ground is ot having to put them away.

As for portable equipment, obtain the best your budget can afford; quality s better than quantity. Use everything you've got, even if it isn't veatherproof. Just remember not to leave wooden pieces out in the rain. When you do store the equipment, keep it together in an accessible spot. Store weatherproof aluminum pieces outside, lashed to a tree with a long hain and a strong lock.

A list included in this article suggests tried and true pieces of equipment, vailable through early childhood mail order catalogs.

Building an Obstacle Course

• Begin at the beginning

A red traffic cone (A) marks the spot where the course begins and ends.

• Obstacle #1—Up

The first obstacle is a walking board (B), sloping gently upward. The losest end rests on the ground; the far end is attached to a sawhorse (C). Some children, like Nathan, will zip up an incline with one fearless ound, while others, like Ana, ascend tentatively, testing the reliability of he board with every step.

Illustration by Lisa Mathias

•Obstacle #2—Over

The second obstacle is straddling the sawhorse. Nathan will step blithely
over it. Ana may crouch, grip the top rung of the sawhorse with both
hands, and back herself carefully over it, until she feels secure.

• Obstacle #3—Down

The third is a descending walking board. Nathan will run or jump down
in a series of bounds; Ana will walk cautiously or will sit, half sliding, half
scooting to the bottom. There is no *one way*. The act of ascending and
descending a sloping walking board can be scary. The receding and
approaching ground beneath young children's feet challenges their
relatively recent sense of equilibrium.

• Obstacle #4—Up

Allow a couple of yards of clear ground so that their momentum will not
send the children crashing into the next obstacle: the first of three
nesting aluminum climbing bridges (D). Ascending the rungs encourages
the use of alternate hands and feet, a valuable exercise for both Ana and
Nathan.

• Obstacle #5—Across

The fifth is an aluminum gangway (E), suspended between level rungs of
the first and second climbing bridges. (Initially, the gangway should be
level; subsequently, it can be slanted for a greater challenge.) If crossing
the open rungs of the gangway appears too difficult, you may lay a
walking board over them. The disadvantage of a solid walkway, however,
is that children tend to congregate on it, stopping the flow of traffic.
Nathan particularly loves to pause on the gangway, waving and calling,
"Hey, guys! Hey down there!"

• Obstacle #6—Down

The next obstacle is the second aluminum bridge. The motor-planning
involved in getting down the rungs is a complicated business. Nathan
prefers to leap from the gangway, eliminating this obstacle altogether.
Ana, like most preschoolers, needs to be helped to turn around so that she
can back down, facing the rungs.

• Obstacle #7—Over

Next comes a tumbling mat (F). Children are inspired by a mat's
resilience and gentle bounciness. Let them discover their favorite form of
locomotion. They may somersault, roll, crawl, or run over the mat. They

may leap up and fall down in an exaggerated heap. Ana likes to tiptoe here. Anything goes.

• Obstacle #8—Through

After the mat comes an obstacle through which to crawl. Crawling is not only for babies; cross-lateral locomotion (whereby opposite arms and legs move forward at the same time) helps to integrate the left and right hemispheres of the brain. When the brain hemispheres are working smoothly together, the whole child functions better, often with noticeable improvements in social behavior, motor skills, and cognitive ability.

Plastic action hoops (G), secured vertically in specially grooved blocks, serve the purpose of a crawl-through obstacle. Hoops are colorful, versatile, and easy to store, but are often knocked down by exuberant children. A sturdier piece of equipment which will invite children to get down on all fours is either a plastic tunnel secured between two panels (H), or a wooden barrel and barrel rack (I) treated for outdoor use.

• Obstacle #9—Across

Two balance beams (J), wide side up, and set parallel to each other, make a novel obstacle. A child who was developmentally delayed, both emotionally and physically, invented this side-by-side set-up because a single balance beam was too frustrating for her. Nathan finds the arrangement very amusing. He often remarks, "Two balance beams? That's so funny!"

• Obstacle #10—Around

Weaving around a series of traffic cones is next. Set down five cones, about 18 inches apart, in a gentle S. To make a serpentine path for the children to follow, sprinkle flour on the ground beside the cones. Flour makes a good path because it is biodegradable, highly visible, and, unlike a rope, stays put. Ana thinks well of this obstacle, saying, "This is like Hansel and Gretel."

• Obstacle #11—Up, Across, and Down

A teetering balance board is the next challenge. Devised by a four year old, this risky looking obstacle is another exercise which helps integrate the left and right brain hemispheres, and thus improve motor and thinking skills.

Center a walking board atop a small wooden triangle (K), as if it were a seesaw. Where each end of the board hits the ground, place a hollow block (L); the blocks will serve to reduce the board's slant.

First, the child inches up the inclined board. Then, he balances momentarily at the fulcrum as his shifting weight causes the board to level. Finally, he runs off the board as it tips downward to strike the block. Many children, like Ana, need a teacher's hand, and will sigh with pride and relief when they return to terra firma. Other children, like Nathan, will want to stand astride the fulcrum and balance, unaided, forever.

• Obstacle #12—Into

More hoops, secured horizontally in their grooved blocks, require another kind of balancing skill. A child must balance on one foot while raising the other foot high in order to step into each hoop. This is not easy for Nathan, but he likes to pretend he is stepping into a boiling cauldron, like the wolf in **The Three Little Pigs**, or into icy cold water, infested by sharks. "Yikes!"

• Obstacle #13—Over

Getting over an inverted rocking boat (M) by stepping up and down the stairs is next.

Photograph by Gail Lynch

• **Obstacle #14—Across**

A single balance beam, wide-side up, is a true challenge. Let the children cross it any way they can—walking as if on a tightrope, sidling, holding a teacher's hand, or with one foot on the ground and the other on the board.

• **Obstacle #15—Through**

A metal crawl tunnel (N) is next. Its open sides and colorful rungs make it an appealing obstacle. Flat on the ground, it invites children either to shimmy forward on their backs, feet first, or to crawl through on their hands and knees. Later, you may raise the tunnel at one end to provide a challenge for either crawling up or sliding down. Nathan, of course, likes it at a rakish tilt.

• **Obstacle #16—Across**

On their feet again, children walk across *stepping stones*. Position tree stumps, hollow blocks, or inverted milk cartons (O) about 4 to 6 inches apart.

• **Obstacle #17—Under**

The last obstacle is the third climbing bridge, placed sideways in the children's path so that they must crouch slightly to pass under it. Because an unattached climbing bridge may be unstable, throw a tent cover (P) or blanket over the rungs to dissuade children from climbing it. Ana likes to spend a cozy moment inside the covered bridge, where she can contemplate her next move.

• **End at the beginning**

Having come full circle, the children meet the solitary red traffic cone which marks the beginning of the course—and they start all over again.

General Guidelines

An obstacle course is addictive; we build one every day. Sure, it takes physical energy to carry wooden rocking boats from shed to playground; but letting the children help works well. To children, putting together a course is not work, but play. It builds muscles and channels energy. Because it requires teamwork and group interaction, it develops social skills. It encourages creative thinking about ways to use equipment, ways grownups wouldn't consider themselves. It strengthens problem-solving skills as children figure out how to incorporate their ideas into the master plan. It involves children as participants rather than spectators. It is, above all, glorious fun!

With the children's guidance, I've learned to build a course neither so difficult that Ana needs a helping hand throughout, nor so simple that Nathan considers it a big bore. Let your students tell you what they want; they know, whereas teachers can only guess.

It is important to be vigilant about safety. Sufficient space between obstacles and stability of equipment are imperative. Check the obstacles frequently to make certain they are secure. If you must leave the site, ask another teacher to take your place, so that a responsible adult is always in attendance.

Avoid giving orders to the children. Do not, for example, insist that everyone do somersaults; the kids won't like it, and neither will you.

Give your slow starters a little extra time before they leap into an obstacle course. Ana likes to watch for a while, to measure how the course is run. She digs her heels in and resists participating if she feels pushed or rushed. She gains confidence, however, if she feels she can join in when she is good and ready. With gentle encouragement, shy children will participate, especially when a trusted teacher is right beside them. Soon they will be able to repeat the course alone, as Ana does, shining with pleasure and crowing, "I did it all by myself!"

To keep the obstacle courses engaging, vary each one by adding and subtracting elements. One day it might be a *Shape Course*, emphasizing squares, triangles, or circles. A *Color-of-the-Day Course* is another variation. On Valentine's Day you may use only red plastic hoops, and apply red arrows and hearts to the walking boards. A *Zigzag Course* provides a different challenge, because changing direction is very hard. Sometimes the course can go indoors instead of outdoors. Sometimes it may become an integral part of enacting a nursery rhyme, such as "Jack and Jill." Let the children try the course barefoot. Or backwards. Or with music. Variations are endless, as no obstacle course design is written in stone.

Once the assembling is over, step back to watch and listen. Success is in the air, for everybody loves an obstacle course, each in a *different* way.

Carol Stock Kranowitz is the music and creative movement teacher at St. Columba's Nursery School in Washington, DC. She is also a household engineer and a free lance writer.

Suggested Equipment

All prices are approximate.

A— Red traffic cones, set of six, $7, Lakeshore Curriculum Materials Co., PO Box 6261, Carson, CA 90749.

B— Walking board, $50, Childcraft, 20 Kilmer Road, Edison, NJ 08818.

C— Sawhorse, $25, Lakeshore.

D— Aluminum climbing bridges, set of three in graduated sizes, $270, Community Playthings, Route 213, Rifton, NY 12471.

E— Aluminum gangway, $115, Community Playthings.

F— Tumbling mat, $125, Childcraft.

G— Plastic action hoops, set of five large hoops and ten grooved hoop holders, $125, Childcraft.

H— "Rotoplay" connecting tunnel and two "Rotoplay" panels, $180, Lakeshore.

I — Barrel and barrel rack, $130, Community Playthings.

J — Balance beam, $50, Childcraft.

K— Variplay Triangle Set, five pieces, $125, Community Playthings.

L— Hollow wooden blocks, introductory set, $165, Community Playthings.

M— Rocking boat, $100, Community Playthings.

N— Crawl tunnel, $200, Playworld Systems, PO Box 227, New Berlin, PA 17855.

O— Lakeshore Huskylight Blocks, $11 (medium) and $15 (large), Lakeshore.

P— Tent cover, $35, Joseph A. Cravero Co., Inc., 315 Broadhollow Road, Route 10, Farmingdale, L.I., NY 11735.

Helping Whole Children Grow: Non-Sexist Childrearing for Infants and Toddlers

by Judith Leipzig

Ask a group of teachers about sex-role stereotyping in the earliest years and most will laughingly respond with "Boys in blue—girls in pink!" or "Trucks for boys—dolls for girls!"—knowing that they would not enforce such codes themselves. It **is** difficult for most of us to identify what might be some of the subtler links between the way we care for babies and toddlers and the limitations and problems experienced by adult men and women. So often it seems as if we interact with babies in response to the individual child, and most teachers would no sooner take a truck away from a toddler girl or steer a baby boy from a doll than they would dress each sex child in a pink or blue uniform. The general sense among most adults is that sex-role stereotyping begins in nursery school or later.

The research during the past few decades can provide us with a lot of food for thought. Most importantly, it may be surprising to learn that no study has conclusively identified any difference between male and female behaviors, activity levels or interests at birth, or in the first two years of life. At the same time, research has substantiated behavioral differences in males and females later in life. This makes it difficult to make a case for the concept that girls or boys behave in a certain way because they're biologically programmed to do so. By the time sex differences do show up, so much has happened to a child which could conceivably have influenced the development of gender typing.

Other research (Moss, 1967; Cherry, 1976; Fagot, 1973; Murphy, 1962) has shown that adults, even those concerned about sex-role stereotyping in later years, do handle male and female babies differently right from the start; and it is probable that this contributes to the very diverse experiences boys and girls have with people, activities, and objects. This, in turn, feeds back into children's self-images, skills, and interests.

A number of studies (Seavey, 1975; Will, 1976; Condry, 1976) sought to discover if this differential handling was in unconscious response to actual sex differences. This research focused on adult interaction with infants, and the adults' interpretation of babies' feelings and communications based on the *perceived* sex of the infant. In these studies, when adults were told that a baby was *male*, they were more likely to see him as sturdy, aggressive, big, angry, and so forth. The same child, when perceived as *female*, was described as delicate, sweet, tiny, frightened, etc. If the study was an interactional one, the adults were more likely to touch, smile at, and talk with the *female baby*, and to hand *her* a doll to play with, while the adults who interacted with the **same** child, but who were told that *he* was a boy, offered the child male stereotyped toys such as a small train.

The Creation of Project Beginning Equal

In 1982, the Pre-School Association, Inc. (PAWS) of New York City approached the New York Community Trust with an idea. PAWS suggested setting up a program that would review the research in child development and sex-role stereotyping, and proceed to develop a series of workshops to help parents and teachers of children under three learn to identify some of the ways in which they pass long this damaging sex-role socialization. Little work had been done to translate this research into action, to identify how to become aware of and change some of our behaviors. The New York Community Trust decided to fund a joint two year project to be conducted by PAWS and the Nonsexist Child Development Project of the Women's Action Alliance, Inc.—an agency with a substantial background in the development of nonsexist curriculum for older children. Out of this collaboration, Project Beginning Equal (BE): The Project on Nonsexist Childrearing for Infants and Toddlers was developed.

The project began with several months of observations and interviews in nine New York City infant/toddler child care centers. Team members had several tasks. First, they noted materials available in the rooms, and who (boys and/or girls) was using them. Second, when team members entered the room for the first time, they immediately attempted to identify which children were male and which female, noting which cues (e.g. dress, hairstyle) might be acting as a gender signal. Later, the observer checked her judgment with the teacher. The results of this exercise followed the pattern concluded by current research: team members could not guess what sex a child was unless one of several signs was apparent—girls sported ornaments and bright colors, while boys wore darker clothing and usually had what little hair they possessed parted on the side.

Arrivals and departures at the center were observed, since interactions between adults and children are often highlighted during these emotional times. In addition, individual observers randomly chose a child and described everything that child did for a period of 15 minutes. The project made use of these observations in the development of workshops, including: "Exploring One's Sex-Role Attitudes"; "Sex-Role Socialization—Adult Interactions with Infants and Toddlers"; "Identifying Conflicts and Developing Strategies for Change"; and "Analyzing Toys for Sex and Race Stereotyping." An additional follow-up workshop, focusing mainly on conflicts with other adults (spouses, other staff, relatives, etc.), was added.

Implications of BE for Early Childhood Programs

It is possible to take the material developed by Project BE and to translate it into our work with children under three in the classroom. Designing a curriculum for children of that age takes a special understanding of how infants and toddlers learn, as well as an awareness of what the real course of study is for very young children. The most important learning in the first years is finding out about the self: what one feels, what one can do, how one fits in, what the world feels like pressed up against and funneled through the self. Without this grounding, all else must be less meaningful. In an educational setting, curriculum for infants and toddlers is really anything a child feels or experiences which is put into a focused and responsive framework for that baby by the staff.

So much of what children learn about themselves and the world comes not through carefully planned activities but through the many repeated everyday encounters that make up a day. What research shows, and the Project BE observations corroborated, is that in general boys and girls have different experiences and are interacted with in distinct ways by adults, based not on actual individual differences, nor even as a result of differences in the child's style, but on the basis of unconscious assumptions made by teachers and parents. These assumptions about children's innate needs, abilities, styles, and futures alter teachers' behaviors drastically, so that girls are learning one curriculum and boys another.

Teachers who want to begin to think about developing their own non-stereotyping curriculum can start with the basic premise that the wider a child's range of experience, both with the self and the outer world, the more likely he or she is to become a well-rounded person. Instead of taking trucks away from the boys, add experience for the boys in the doll corner. Instead of taking art projects away from the girls, add some exciting gross motor play. Children need opportunities for exploring different kinds of relationships with people, materials, and activities. They need the chance to incorporate information about closeness *and* separateness, about assertiveness *and* cooperation.

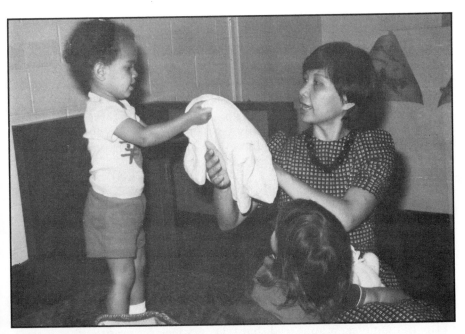

Photograph by Subjects and Predicates

Patterns in Adult-Child Interactions

As the specialist in infant and parent development with the Project BE
team, it was my job to review the 70 plus observations collected by the
team members. These anecdotes suggested to me a number of patterns
about adult-child interactions. It is important to note that these
hypotheses are not the result of actual research, but are questions and
ideas gleaned from the observations which follow the path identified by
actual research studies. As teachers, it can be useful to use these
hypotheses to begin to view our own behavior with a more critical eye.

*Two year old Luis and 20 month old Alma are crying for their mothers.
Two caregivers approach them warmly: "Hey, Luis honey," says the first.
"Did you see the new red blocks we got for the block corner? Come on,
let's go take a look." The other adult takes Alma in her arms, saying, "I
know you're feeling sad because you're missing your mommy. She's gone
to work, but she'll be back after lunch. It'll be okay. I'm gonna take good
care of you."*

This observation reflects the sense that boys were generally steered away
from experiencing their feelings, while girls were supported in exploring
theirs. Teachers encouraged boys to find something to do or play with
when they were sad, but talked to, cuddled, and articulated the girls'
experiences for them. In the story above, Alma's caregiver is providing

her with some very important information: Alma learns that the important adult both recognizes her feelings and respects them. She begins to put together a more coherent picture of her inner turmoil— among other things, Alma is learning that there are names for these feelings (sad and missing); there is a reason for them (mommy has gone away); and the occasion for the sadness has a limit (it will end after lunch). Luis, on the other hand, has his most intense emotional experience blanked out. It certainly seems possible that this difference in handling could make a contribution to the difficulty many adult men experience in connecting with their feelings.

By 11 a.m. the floor of the child care center is strewn with the remains of some very intense playing. "Clean up time," calls the teacher. "We've got to get ready to go outside. Here, Lucy, you can help me find all the red Legos, now all the blue ones. Can you put them in this box? Terrific, you're really doing a good job!" As the teacher works with 15 month old Lucy, she glances over at a cluster of two year old boys who are already pulling their coats out of their cubbies. "Really, it's more trouble than it's worth to try to get the boys to help with clean up."

In the BE samples, it appeared that teachers took for granted that girls should be learning to be aware of their environment and to take some responsibility in cleaning up, setting the table for lunch, and so forth. They devised interesting ways to help the girl toddlers begin to be socialized in this way. In contrast, they failed to pursue this area of curriculum with the boys. Those teachers who did call out a general announcement for clean-up usually did not give the boys the support and encouragement needed to develop skills in this area. Instead, boys were left to continue playing or to drift aimlessly. One wonders what connection this lack of social learning has with the general unawareness, lack of skill, and lack of personal responsibility many adult men have when it comes to caring for their home environment.

Twelve month old Carla has been getting ready to walk on her own. This morning, with a look of great concentration, she struggles to take her first steps. She crows in triumph as she toddles toward the caregiver. "Oh, Carla! Don't you look pretty! Hey, cute thing—look at you strutting your stuff!" exclaims one caregiver. Another adult says, "Doesn't she look so sweet with those pretty lace panties wiggling along?"

Often girls were complimented on their appearance, boys on their achievements. Even when baby girls were achieving important milestones, it was their appearance that was commented on. In the example above, the responses of the caregivers, though warm and excited, were actually missing the point of what the experience was for this child. Instead of cheering on her first steps, exclaiming over her new motor abilities, her competence, her maturity, the teachers emphasized for

Carla how appealing, how accessible, and even possibly how sexy she was to others. A 12 month old boy walking for the first time might have heard "Yay! Good walking! Look at that big guy—good for you!"—that is, the most salient aspect of his experience would have been noted. The thrust seems to be that boys are encouraged to do things as a response to their own inner drives, interests and development, and that adults value the achievement in terms of its meaning for the child.

Again, we can think about the implications for later life. Many adult women struggle to identify what they actually want to achieve for themselves, since part of female socialization makes it difficult for women to see their own needs and interests separate from the desires and priorities of others. One could hypothesize that this turning of achievement into a chance to be attractive and pleasing to others might contribute to this facet of female development.

In one center, eight month old Brian begins to cry. Marian, a caregiver, picks him up and cuddles him to no avail. She changes his diaper, offers him a bottle; all of which have no effect on the crying. Marian and her co-teacher become increasingly concerned, attempting one thing after another to figure out what might be going on—realizing that Brian's crying has meaning and is communicating a need that ought to be met.

In another center 11 month old Rebecca is urgently tugging at her special cuddly bear which is caught under a rocking chair. Adult caregivers come and go, passing by Rebecca and the chair as they attend to their duties. Rebecca begins to whimper and crawls under the chair, looking for a way to retrieve her bear. She looks from bear to adult and back, whimpering loudly. Lois, a teacher, gives Rebecca an affectionate pat on the head and continues reading to another child. Finally, Rebecca beings to howl loudly in frustration. "What's the matter with Rebecca?" asks Lois. "Oh, she's probably had it with being inside all morning," answers David. Rebecca is swooped up and carried to the door. No one has taken a moment to focus on what this child may be communicating.

These two anecdotes exemplify the way adults tend to miss the cues of pre-verbal girls more frequently than of pre-verbal boys. Teachers attempted to decode the communications and gestures of the infant boys more consistently in the Project BE observations; in fact, they often did not even notice that a baby girl had expressed a desire or need.

In addition, observers noted that male toddlers were allowed to wander around the room, generally able to follow their own internal schedules and interests, collecting important information about people and things as they cruised through space. Female toddlers, in contrast, were frequently interrupted in their explorations. The girls were more consistently required to curtail or interrupt their self-motivated activities to respond to the teacher's schedule or needs. In behavioral terms, it may look something like this: a little girl who is concentrating on the challenges of a shape-sorting box is interrupted from her work by a teacher who swoops the child up suddenly for a hug. In another illustration of this dynamic, a teacher decides it is time to change a girl's diaper or take her for a walk, and immediately acts on her decision, even though the girl toddler is engrossed in water play. The child is not permitted the few moments needed to feel a sense of completion. Baby girls were not responded to in ways that support the growth of a sense of personal effectiveness, a sense that one can order and cope with the environment. Adult women often have difficulty maintaining an image of themselves as an effective person—as a person who can decide on a goal, form a plan of action, and then *go for it.* Without this feeling, it's much harder to create a life of one's own.

The teacher is sitting on the floor with two little boys while they play with the Bristle Blocks. As the boys build, she uses herself as a focusing and grounding presence by simply being there, commenting on their work, mentioning the colors, the textures, the ideas. Over to the side, a girl toddler sits, watching all the activity wistfully, turning a single Bristle Block over and over in her hands.

Photograph by Michael Siluk

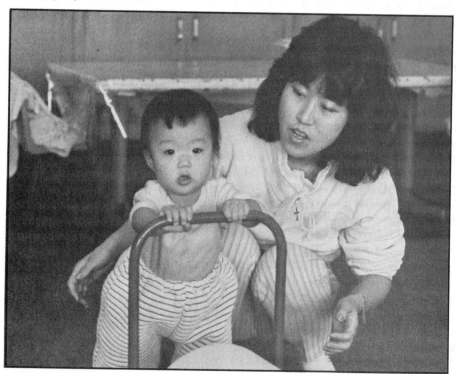

Another group of BE observations seemed to point to the hypothesis that teachers view onlooking girls as participants. If a girl was watching an activity, teachers were much less likely to try to draw her into the activity, much less likely to help her have a hands-on experience, than they would be with a boy. Teachers usually interpret a boy's interest as an interest to be *doing*, and help the child find his way into the activity. Girls miss some of those important learning experiences because teachers view the girls' observing as sufficient participation. In the story above, the boys were learning (to name a few) about how to work together, to develop their ideas, to concentrate, information about spatial relationships, fine motor skills, and color. The experiences that children have in the early years are the foundational blocks upon which later learning and compe-tencies are built. Those adults who have had the opportunity to develop basic skills and collect this information early on are better equipped to learn what they need in order to function in our complex and demanding world. If little girls are short changed in this respect, adult women may suffer.

Conclusion

Since we are the most important tools of our curriculum concepts, it is mandatory for us to observe ourselves, to review our personal assumptions about children, and to repeatedly help each other shake free of these biases. The teachers that Project BE observed were for the most part caring and responsible people; but like all of us, they were often acting on unconscious assumptions that we have all been taught. Much more important than what we directly say to the infants and toddlers in our care are these many daily personal interactions and the messages they impress on the individual child. When a child receives messages— either directly through words and gestures, or less directly through assumptions and fantasies adults have about the child—that child is absorbing a picture of what is possible, what is permissible, and what is to be. When we talk about sexist childrearing, we're talking about something that goes far beyond isolated and superficial pieces of behavior, far beyond dressing girls in pink and boys in blue. This kind of experience becomes a lens through which children will see the world and themselves.

As educators of very young people who are in the midst of creating their selves and their futures, it is our responsibility to think about what kinds of raw materials we are providing them. Each child should have the support, the attention, and the experiences that will help that child grow to be a competent, well-rounded, and loving person—one who has a clear picture of his or her self, one who is able to cooperate and to work on her or his own, and one who is able to both give and receive support and nurturing. As teachers of infants and toddlers, we should be doing everything in our power to support the development of individuals who will be capable of leading rich and balanced lives.

References

Cherry, L., and M. Lewis. "Mothers of Two Year Olds: A Study of Sex Differentiated Aspects of Verbal Interaction," **Merrill-Palmer Quarterly** 13, 1976.

Condry, J., and S. Condry. "Sex Differences: A Study of the Eye of the Beholder," **Child Development**, 47, 1976.

Fagot, B. I. "Sex-Related Stereotyping of Toddler Behaviors," **Developmental Psychology**, 9, 1973.

Maccoby, E. E., and D. N. Jacklin. **The Psychology of Sex Differences.** Stanford, CA: Stanford University Press, 1974.

Moss, H. A. "Sex, Age and State as Determinants of Mother-Infant Interaction," **Merrill-Palmer Quarterly**, 13, 1967.

Murphy, L. B. **The Widening World of Childhood.** New York: Basic Books, 1962.

Seavey, C. A., et al. "Baby X: The Effect of Gender Labels on Adult Responses to Infants," **Sex Roles**, 1, 1975.

Will, J. A., et al. "Maternal Behavior and Perceived Sex of Infant," **American Journal of Orthopsychiatry**, 46, 1976.

Women's Action Alliance, Inc. and the Pre-School Association, Inc. **Beginning Equal: A Manual About Nonsexist Childrearing For Infants and Toddlers.** New York: Women's Action Alliance, 1983.

Judith Leipzig is a specialist in infant and parent development. Currently she teaches at Bank Street College of Education in New York City.

Checklist for Self-Observation

Before you start to make changes, take a week to begin to observe yourself in your interactions with children. The following questions may be helpful in organizing your observations:

1. Look around the room several times a day. Are boys only playing with gross motor toys and blocks? Are girls only in the housekeeping corner or at the fine motor table? Do you personally spend little time in areas traditionally labeled for the other sex?

2. Observe the way you handle times of emotional stress for boys and for girls. Are you unconsciously distracting boys from their feelings while you give girls support for and language to describe their distress?

3. Notice what happens during clean up times. Who helps? Does your staff try to think of imaginative ways to involve most of the children who are old enough to participate?

4. Watch carefully and note repeatedly the way you talk. Are you aware of the language you use with children? What do you focus on to praise about little girls? about little boys? Observe yourself carefully to see what you applaud, or even comment on, and what the underlying messages might be that you are sending with the words you choose.

5. Think before you interrupt any child. Ask yourself: Is it necessary? What is the child experiencing right now? How can I give him or her time to complete this and still get my work done?

6. Compare your responses to a few of the baby girls and a few of the baby boys to see if there are different patterns of care. Are you noticing the communications of pre-verbal girls? When you do notice them, do you put effort into deciphering their meaning? It may be helpful for staff members to take turns sitting on the sidelines and trying to write down more objective observations, since it's often easier to notice behaviors when one is unencumbered and uninvolved.

7. Take a look at how the children are engaged in their play. Do all children actively participate in what's going on in the room? How often are there children sitting on the periphery of an activity for long periods of time, showing interest but not able to actually join in? What sex are they?

Lost in a Distant Land: The Foreign Child's Dilemma in Child Care

by Athol B. Packer, Sharon C. Milner, and Marion H. Hong

An Oriental mother and her three year old son, who speak very little English, approach the center's front door. When the child's mother encourages him to enter, his whine turns into a loud wail. Some children stop playing and stare at him. A teacher stops her planning work and tries to draw the child into the classroom activities. After 30 minutes this young mother is still by the door; whenever she turns and tries to walk away, her child follows and clings to her leg.

For a minute, try to put yourself in a similar situation. Imagine yourself in a foreign country where you don't speak the language and the natives do not speak English. In such a predicament you might feel considerable anxiety and discomfort. Just satisfying your basic needs—getting a drink of water or finding a bathroom—can cause problems. You feel lost and disoriented, cut off from natural means of communication. Those who have traveled in a foreign country can certainly relate to these circumstances.

Non-English speaking children placed in a child care center face much the same situation. They are in a foreign country, a land of giant adults who speak a strange language. For many of these children, this is their first separation from their parents. To help these children adjust to new experiences, it is necessary to become more sensitive to their particular needs. Foreign families have special problems adjusting to child care. This article describes a program developed to aid foreign children, their parents, and their teachers.

Thirty-three three and four year old children from foreign countries were enrolled for full time child care at the University of Florida's Baby Gator Educational Research Center for Child Development in August 1986. The children and their families came from 20 countries—including Brazil, Venezuela, Costa Rica, Korea, China, Iran, Egypt, India, Israel, Poland, Malaysia, Bangladesh, Cameroon, and South Africa. The high percentage of foreign children results from our center being located on the University of Florida campus. Our student population includes a substantial number of married foreign students with children. The majority of preschool centers in the United States might typically have only a few non-English speaking children from other countries.

Thirty-five foreign children out of a total of 105 in a child care center. What are the implications for children, parents, and staff?

• Separation anxiety of young foreign children is heightened by their inability to communicate adequately with peers and teachers.

• Parents, especially the mothers of young foreign children, have special needs and concerns that need to be addressed, such as lack of confidence and security about the center, perhaps reluctance to use a new language.

• Teachers experience stresses and frustrations in working with these families and their particular needs in addition to all their other responsibilities.

How are the children affected?

Foreign children may experience anxiety and fear beyond that of other children because they lack the language skills to communicate their needs. For example, the child may say, "I need to go to the bathroom" in his/her language. A teacher not knowing the child's language might think the child is asking for a drink of water or to go outside and play. It can be very frustrating to the child not to be understood. Fortunately, these young children pick up nonverbal cues from English speakers which eliminate many communication fears, and they are also quick to use their own body language to fill in the gaps. Because everything may be so different in the center, it can be especially difficult for these children to develop a sense of belonging.

What are the parents feeling?

The foreign parent may feel as lost and lonely in our country as her child does. She may be anxious about the welfare of her child because she is unable to talk easily about her concerns. She may be hesitant even to try asking the staff about the program or what her child does all day in the center. Even when the staff provides her a schedule of the daily activities, terms such as *free play, cubbie*, and *circle time* may be unfamiliar to her.

Foreign parents who place their children in a child care center may also be suffering from separation anxiety. The staff can comfort them by saying, "It's okay to feel bad and a little anxious when you are leaving your child for the first time." Just recognizing and acknowledging that you understand their feelings about leaving their child may be all that is needed to relieve their anxiety. They can also be encouraged to stay and observe; some of what may be difficult to communicate verbally can be learned by just watching what goes on in the program. Efforts to help parents deal with their feelings will pay big dividends for parents and children and will make the center's work easier and more effective.

What is the impact on the teachers?

At the beginning of the school year, teachers are faced with a multitude of tasks to accomplish. Lesson plans must be prepared. Teaching materials must be gathered. The room must be organized. New children, in fact, all children, must be welcomed and helped to feel comfortable and secure. Teachers must also communicate with parents to help them feel secure. These teacher tasks can seem overwhelming. Add to this the particular needs of several non-English speaking children and their parents, and teachers may feel that it's more than they can handle. Teachers, as well as the children and their parents, need help in adjusting to working together in the program.

What can be done to help the children adjust?

The child care center has to take an active role in developing and implementing strategies to aid the adjustment of foreign parents and children. The following strategies have worked in our center:

Photograph by Bonnie Neugebauer

Teachers are encouraged to maintain eye contact when talking to non-English-speaking children and to be aware of the child's nonverbal body language. Because words for objects and actions that can be displayed or demonstrated are much easier to learn for children, teachers are encouraged to speak slightly slower with gestures and visual cues.

A list of common terms and functioning words that children frequently use in a child care program was compiled by the teachers and the research assistant. The terms are translated into Spanish, Chinese, and Korean—the languages representing the majority of non-English speaking children enrolled. (It is suggested that your program provide translations into other languages spoken by families in your center.) A brochure containing this list is given to foreign parents when they enroll their children. Parents are encouraged to talk about these words at home so that they become familiar to the child. Several other familiar words and phrases such as *share, What is your name?, My name is____, and Thank you* are often found to be important.

It is also helpful for teachers to make an effort to communicate with children in their native language; even just a few words in a child's language can be comforting. Cassette tapes and simple versions of foreign language phonetic transcriptions are made for teachers to learn the pronunciation of the terms in the child's language.

When new foreign children arrive in school, teachers are encouraged to provide a *bilingual buddy* to add to the children's security. If there is another child who speaks the same language as the new child, this bilingual friend can help as both translator and person to identify with to help ease the transition.

Guidelines for Parents

Sometimes foreign parents are not aware that they are able to participate in local parent education classes, or they may not know about local services such as the public library and health clinic. Some mothers fear that their English is not fluent enough. This makes them reluctant to become involved in the community or join in the center's parental involvement program. Parents may also be unsure what will help their children adjust and learn to communicate. Our brochure includes guidelines for parents to enhance their children's language and social adjustment:

• Encourage children to play with English-speaking children to enhance their language development.

• Encourage children to watch selected television programs (**Mr. Rogers, Captain Kangaroo, Sesame Street**) to enrich their social background.

• Teach children basic safety rules:

Beware of strangers.
Only take medicines and food from mom, dad, or teachers.
Keep small objects out of eyes, ears, and nose.
Stay out of the street.
Use words to solve problems, not hitting.

• Check out children's books from the library:

Going to Day Care by Fred Rogers (New York: G. P. Putnam Sons, 1985).
I Can Build A House by Shigeo Watanabe (New York: Putnam Publishing Group, 1982).
The Other Bone by Ed Young (New York: Harper and Row, Publishers, 1984).
Naptime by Gylbert Coker (New York: Delacorte Press, 1978).
Geraldine's Blanket by Holly Keller (New York: Greenwillow Books, 1984).
Whistle For Willie by Ezra Jack Keats (New York: The Viking Press, 1964).
Snow by Isao Sasaki (New York: The Viking Press, 1980).
A Tasting Party by Jane Belk Moncure (Chicago: Children's Press, 1982).
The Very Hungry Caterpillar by Eric Carle (New York: Philomel Books, 1982).

• Check out story tapes from the library (in both English and your own language).

• Read to them in your native language.

• Become involved in your child's school as a teacher supporter or by helping with a special project.

• Participate in local parenting groups or English classes.

Guidelines for Teachers

Teachers and children will do best when the atmosphere is relaxed and non-threatening. Body language can take care of many basic communications, and teachers need to remind themselves that children will learn English quickly and naturally.

When developing learning activities, teachers should draw on the children's family and cultural backgrounds and personal interests. High interest, fun activities such as finger plays and songs appeal to children across language barriers. Good illustrations help children understand the activity even though they may not comprehend all the words they hear.

Classroom displays including objects or art familiar to the child, familiar foods at snack, a favorite story all help the child feel that he belongs.

International potluck dinners can enhance the multicultural awareness of all the children and their families.

A foreign parents' orientation meeting can help parents and teachers get to know each other better. Teachers can learn about parents' expectations for their children in the program, and parents can find out about the program's philosophy. In the past, parents have expressed appreciation for such special interest and concern. This orientation provides an opportunity for parents to express their concerns, thereby building their confidence and security about the center. When parents demonstrate this confidence, their children appear to adjust more easily and feel more secure in the program.

Conclusion

It is a fact of American society that many cultures actively function within and alongside the mainstream. A sensitive caregiver will recognize this and provide these children with security and a comfortable setting. Furthermore, children in general will benefit from this multicultural involvement. We are excited about the results of our program, and we believe that these strategies can act as a model and catalyst for the development of related child care programs. These strategies can facilitate better adjustment of foreign parents and children in the present and deeper international understanding in the future.

If you are interested in receiving a copy of the brochure for parents and teachers of young bilingual children mentioned in this article, "Words Children Need at Preschool," send a self-addressed, stamped envelope to Athol Packer, College of Education, 2207 Norman Hall, University of Florida, Gainesville, FL 32611.

Athol Packer is an associate professor in early childhood education at the University of Florida, Gainesville. Sharon Milner is on leave from her position as director of Baby Gator and is teaching at the American School in Amsterdam, Holland. Marion Hong is a research assistant and doctoral student at the University of Florida.

Common Terms Used in Child Care

eat	telephone
hungry	free play
water	clean up time
lunch time	rug time/story time
snack time	activity time
happy	nap time
sad	wake up time
quiet	pick up time
listen	good touches/warm fuzzy
look	go to the bathroom/potty
hurt	wash hands
sit down	go inside
hold hands	go outside
toy	come here
cubbie	sick/I do not feel well

Photograph by Subjects and Predicates

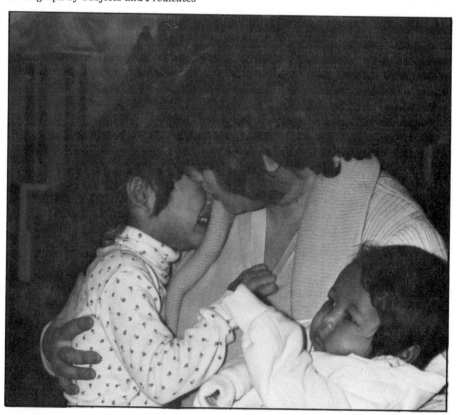

Guidelines for Helping Non-English Speaking Children Adjust and Communicate

by Karen Miller

• Build Trust

The child needs you now. You are his *safe place*. As much as is practical, make yourself available for special holding. Although the child may not understand your words, he will understand eye contact, smiles, reassuring touches. Once the child feels safe, he will begin to venture out, but you are definitely the starting point.

• Learn Key Words

Learn some key words and phrases in the child's language. Ask parents how the child will tell you she needs to go to the bathroom, she's tired, she's hungry, etc.

• Be a Good Language Model

Speak slowly and clearly in a normal tone of voice. Use complete sentences. Extend single word utterances of the child: When he says, "Shoes," say, "Yes, I see you have new red shoes on today."

• Build Receptive Language

Children will be able to understand things you say to them long before they will be able to say words or express themselves to you in words. This is receptive language or understanding.

Talk a lot. Describe what you are doing, what the child is doing. Talk to the child as though he understands you, and then help him understand you by helping him do what you are talking about. "Masafumi, it's time to go to the table to eat lunch." Then take him by the hand, lead him over to the table, and sit down with him.

Photograph by Judy Burr

• Encourage Productive Language

Young children's brains are programmed to absorb language. They will pick up English very quickly. Often the first words a child says out loud are the social words: *hi, good morning, bye, thank you;* also *yes, no,* and *okay.* Encourage all the children to say "Hi" or "Good morning" when other children come in in the morning. Always say "Please" and "Thank you." You will be surprised how quickly these words come, and with what pride.

• Try to Understand Nonverbal Communication

Read the child's nonverbal communication and supply the words. The child points to the pitcher and grunts. "Oh, you want more juice? I'll be glad to pour you some juice." You are acting as an interpreter for the child, connecting useful words to feelings. "Maria is sad because she can't find her hat."

• **Encourage Interactions**

As the child builds a sense of trust with you, help her interact with other children. This will not only help her social adjustment, but it will provide her with opportunities to hear English and to practice.

• **Read Books Together**

Read books that are familiar to the child over and over. Wordless picture books are valuable, as are stories with predictable outcomes and repetitive patterns.

• **Listen and Dance to Music**

Music touches us in a way all people understand. An inconsolable child might be comforted by some gentle singing from you. Songs with repeated phrases are good to use. "Ee-ei-ee-ei-o" is easy to master and fun to sing. Singing is much easier than talking because the words usually come out slower and are more predictable; it's good practice for productive language.

• **Provide Open-Ended Activities**

Just like all other children, your non-English speaking children will need many experiences of success to develop a feeling of self-worth. Try to arrange many open-ended, creative experiences for the child. Provide interesting materials, and anything the child comes up with is fine. Play dough, water play, easel painting, manipulatives, and dramatic play are ideal open-ended activities, and they provide many concrete opportunities for language as well.

• **Use Appropriate Discipline Techniques**

Whatever the child's culture or language, the discipline needs are the same. Children need firm, gentle guidance and consistent limits. Sometimes children will pretend not to understand your reprimands long after they really do understand. Remember that the nonverbal messages of a discipline situation are always understood, so make your tone of voice and facial expression match your words. If a child takes a toy from another child, simply get down on the child's level, hold her shoulders, look into her eyes, and say firmly, "No, that's not okay." Use the same techniques you use with the other children of praising good behavior and redirecting unacceptable behavior.

• Let the Children Teach

Encourage the child to teach you and the other children some words in his language. Make a book using these new words. Use the child's language and culture to redo the housekeeping corner. Let the child teach a song or game. Learn to count in her language. Invite the parents to share a tradition or cooking lesson, to read a familiar book in their language, or to share a different clothing style.

• Exchange Pictures

Ask parents to bring in pictures of their family, family celebrations, former home, etc. to display in the center. Send pictures of you and the children home with the child. Such photo exchanges foster a sense of belonging.

This material is adapted from an article written by Karen Miller for the Children's World Staff Newsletter, November 1986, and is based largely on the experiences of Ana Arista, teacher of three year olds at the Children's World center at St. Paul Hospital in Dallas, Texas.

Recognizing Giftedness
in
Early Childhood Settings

by Donna Garnett Chitwood

Three year old Justin had been the subject of discussion among the teachers in his preschool for several months. He was a highly verbal, active, curious child who spent hours conversing with the adults in the room but rarely interacted with age peers. Activity times that were relatively unstructured were appealing to him, but he never seemed to pay attention in circle time. He would lie on the floor rolling back and forth, playing with his fingers or clothing, looking around at everything but the teacher, and even sometimes humming softly to himself.

On one particular day one of his teachers sat down to observe the circle and Justin, so that she could better talk to his parents about his behavior problems. She carefully recorded his behavior and the activities going on in the group interaction.

Several hours after circle, the teacher had an opportunity to discuss with Justin the events and circumstances of the group activity earlier in the day. Not expecting a knowledgeable response, she, nevertheless, proceeded to ask the youngster about his experience. First she asked him to tell her about the circle time. In response he recounted the story that had been read and sang a ten verse song that had been introduced for the first time that day. She then asked him what he was doing while the teacher was talking, to which he replied, "Listening."

Taking her investigation a step further, the teacher queried, "What were the other children doing during circle today?" Justin responded by describing where each of the 15 other children had been sitting, what they had said to the teacher and each other, who got in trouble, who didn't sing, and so on. In utter awe, his teacher concluded that the parent conference had best focus on his exceptional abilities and how to better accommodate those for his optimum development.

Photograph by Subjects and Predicates

Justin's story is indicative of the nature of some gifted children who exhibit a different learning style from the mainstream of normal children. It was not until three years later that is was discovered that Justin had auditory processing problems and that his unusual way of *listening* was his way of compensating. Fortunately, his preschool teacher had taken the time to observe and try to understand his behavior instead of just immediately categorizing him as a problem and punishing him for his *acting out.*

Tanisha was a charming little four year old girl. She loved coming to school and joyfully went about the business of doing all the planned activities and then spending time in the dramatic play area directing her friends in elaborate dramas. She enjoyed creative art and spent hours drawing and painting her representations of the world.

Soon her teacher began to notice that she was writing words to go along with her artwork—not just three and four letter words—but more descriptive ones like "pepperoni pizza" and "acrimonious." It was also becoming apparent that Tanisha was reading—as her dramatic play turned toward playing school and she gathered her friends around to read stories to them.

Tanisha's exceptional abilities are easier to spot in the early childhood setting because they deviate so obviously from the normal developmental expectation and because they deviate in such a positive manner. For most teachers she is a delight, and very little has to be done with her because she is compliant and pleasant.

The dangerous aspect of Tanisha's case is that as a girl she is likely to be socialized to hide her giftedness by the time she is in third grade. Much support for Tanisha and encouragement to not go underground will be necessary in her early grades. Her parents will need encouragement to pursue appropriate educational experiences for their daughter. There will be the temptation to sit back and accept her schooling experience because she will do so well—so well, in fact, that she will disguise those abilities that threaten her acceptance by peers and teachers.

Another type of giftedness that is difficult to identify in the early childhood setting is the type that is buried within the exterior of an introverted, withdrawn child. This child's capabilities are difficult to observe because he or she doesn't readily verbalize perceptions of the world. This child might even be classified as *socially immature* because he doesn't relate easily to his peers and prefers adult conversation over playing with his agemates.

Mario was just such a child. In the year that he had been in the preschool, he still didn't enthusiastically demand his turn during sharing time, and he still needed half an hour or more to warm up to the situation each day. During free play he usually chose solitary activities from the manipulative or science areas or followed one of the teachers around engaging her in conversation. The teachers often remarked that he was three going on 30, yet in parent conferences his social immaturity was always the topic of discussion.

The summer when he was four the preschool offered a special workshop for young gifted children. At his parents' insistence he was screened for the class, and through the skilled assessment made by the evaluating teacher, Mario was identified in the highly gifted range. During the summer workshop, Mario had ample opportunity to interact with other children who operated on the same level as he. There were very loose time constraints, so that there was still plenty of time to be involved after he had taken his normal warm-up time.

That summer he developed a special relationship with two other children as they constructed a river system in the sand pit that was complete with terraces, logging camp, and dams. The teacher was amazed when one day she overheard a conversation among the three young engineers as they discussed the premise behind hydraulic energy! When allowed the time he needed to trust the environment and ensured that he had other children to relate to on his own cognitive level, Mario didn't look so immature.

As may be seen by these three examples, giftedness is manifest in a variety of different ways. As with any other exceptional learning need, the earlier such need is identified, the better chances are that the child will get and respond to appropriate stimulation. As with all young children, a primary concern is the development of a healthy attitude about oneself and one's abilities. Taking the time to identify the young gifted child and trying to accommodate his or her special learning needs is absolutely critical to the development of that healthy attitude.

Identifying Characteristics of Gifted Preschoolers

The first step in identification is to listen to the parents. Interestingly, studies show that when given specific criteria, parents are the best identifiers of their child's giftedness. Parents have observed their child's development over time and have usually built a safe enough environment for the child to exhibit his or her special abilities. Early childhood teachers can assist parents by becoming aware themselves of the characteristics of the young gifted child.

The Silverman/Waters Checklist for Identifying Giftedness provides a good guide for recognizing the characteristics associated with giftedness. These include:

• **Good problem solving abilities**—may be problems involving things, people, or events.

• **Rapid learning ability**—for some things the child may pick up the relevant elements after hearing or seeing one demonstration. This child will be bored with the repetition typical of most preschool programs.

• **Extensive vocabulary**—uses language with great facility to describe and process the environment. Three year old Jesse astounded his teachers by explaining the "big bang theory of the creation of the universe" after the group had sung a song about ten little rockets.

• **Good memory**—will be able to remember events from months or even years before. Lisa once surprised her mother by asking if she could have a pinata for her birthday like the one Brian had for his party. Brian's party had been over a year ago, and Lisa had only been 18 months old when she watched the pinata breaking.

• **Long attention span**—especially for things that he or she finds of great interest. Some gifted children can work at a specific task in which they are interested for hours.

• **Sensitivity**—may get feelings hurt easily or may be exceptionally tuned in to others' nonverbal communications.

• **Compassion for others**—may exhibit an unusual sensitivity to other adults, children, or animals. At four and a half, Austin listened intently as the newscaster explained how a baby chimpanzee's heart had been transplanted into a very ill newborn human baby. He then turned to his mother and said, "That means that the baby chimpanzee died." Before she could respond, he tearfully queried, "Why is it okay for a baby human to live and a baby chimpanzee to die?"

• **Perfectionism**—not necessarily in all areas, but in performance areas may be reluctant to take risks for fear of failing.

• **High degree of energy**—may have considerably less need for sleep than others, possibly dropped naps during early toddlerhood.

• **Preference for older companions**—enjoys the challenge of relating to older children and adults.

• **Wide range of interests**—usually interested in a great variety of subjects from dinosaurs to politics to trees and more.

• **Excellent sense of humor**—because of an advanced intellectual capacity is able to see the absurdity of life, and particularly enjoys play on words.

• **Early or avid reading ability**—may actually become a self-taught reader at three or four years or at least show a marked interest in being read to even from infancy.

• **Ability in puzzles, mazes, or numbers**—shows unusual ability in working difficult puzzles at early age or like Mark is able to add and subtract two digit numbers by five and have a complete fascination with the notion of negative numbers.

• **At times seems mature for age**—may have areas of development that almost seem delayed by comparison to the intellectual ability. Jessica could actually be left in charge of a small group of children if the teacher had to leave the room for a few moments.

• **Perseverance**—in areas of interest the child may continue with a project that is unusually difficult and frustrating. Theresa worked for several days to complete a sewing project that she had designed. Her four year old fingers had a difficult time matching the designs of her thoughts.

Children who fit 10 out of the 16 characteristics are very possibly gifted.

Testing for Giftedness

The second step in identification is to assist the parents in locating the appropriate type of testing (if necessary). In many states, special educational experiences for gifted children are not available until third grade. However, as with any special learning need, it is vital to have a clear picture of the situation as early as possible. Testing and assessment conducted by a trained professional can contribute greatly to a better understanding of the child. It is preferable that such assessment include an individual intelligence test, observations, and interviews with the parents.

For some parents, going through the testing procedure will ease their minds and help give perspective to the frustrations they have felt about parenting this special child. Although most parents of identified gifted preschoolers are pleased initially with the testing outcome, they very quickly become almost depressed about the burden of parenting a special needs child. Support groups for parents and other opportunities to discuss their feelings and frustrations are especially beneficial at this time.

Providing Appropriate Learning Experiences

Lastly, it is important that the child have the most appropriate experiences possible while still in the preschool environment.

• The young gifted child needs the opportunity to interact with other children who are at the same cognitive level. Therefore, a mixed age grouping can be especially beneficial for these children.

• The curriculum should allow for multilevel response and be challenging in a variety of ways. The young gifted child (as any other preschooler) does not need to spend hours completing workbook pages. Rather, a more appropriate approach is to provide more exploratory types of experiences with ample time to delve deeper into areas of special interest. Programs that focus on individualized planning and discovery models will be particularly suitable for the gifted child.

• As with all young children, focus on self-concept should be primary. The teacher must offer a safe environment in which the gifted child is able to overcome some of the perfectionism that accompanies giftedness and be able to try new experiences. Forcing the child to try something new will not be helpful, but rather patience and a sensitivity as to the conditions under which the child will try will be helpful. Providing an environment where right answers are not expected but rather where many possible answers exist will also be more appropriate.

• It is critical that the child's social immaturities not become a penalizing factor to his/her cognitive abilities. Preventing an extremely bright child from entering kindergarten because he or she is not ready socially may only make that gap seem larger in the future.

• Gifted children are rarely gifted in all areas, and the discrepancies between cognitive development and physical development are often sources of great frustration as the three year old body refuses to accomplish what the five year old mind conceptualizes. Adults must provide encouragement without placing adult standards on the products created, and they can show shortcuts over some difficult areas. For example, the adult can write down the creative story told by the youngster rather than insisting that she laboriously write her own words. Another option might be to show her how to work a tape recorder so she can record her own story.

Working with gifted children in the early childhood years can be a gratifying experience for teachers. However, it is critical that it be recognized that giftedness comes in many different forms and that not all of those children will look like Tanisha. The different needs of all young children must be considered and appropriate experiences must be facilitated to accommodate those individual differences.

Donna Garnett Chitwood is the director of the child care division at Auraria Higher Education Center in Denver, Colorado. She works with parents and teachers to identify giftedness in young children and to plan appropriate educational experiences for these children.

Exploring Diversity Through the Arts

interviews with Jimena Lasansky and Richard Lewis by Susan Epeneter, interview with Bob Blue by Candace Chang

Question: Poetry, storytelling, music, movement, dance—what do these different art forms have to contribute to a discussion of diversity?

Answer: Each can be used to broaden children's views and understandings of the world and its inhabitants. Artists involved in working with children in three different art forms were asked a series of questions regarding how the arts can be used to broaden children's perceptions of the world at large and the people, both like and unlike themselves, who inhabit that world. Each artist also offered suggestions for early childhood teachers in working to accomplish understanding and acceptance in children.

Jimena Lasansky is a professional dancer and choreographer and part-time professor of dance at the University of Maine in Augusta. She currently tours extensively, performing and conducting master classes and creative movement workshops for children and adults.

Jimena Lasansky: My focus is on dance, but my ultimate goal, of course, is not to create a multitude of dancers, but to help children communicate issues they have within themselves. The beauty of dance is that dance is a universal way to communicate. In dance, in movement, in gesture, there are feelings. I can sit with a group and say, "Tell me something with your hands or with your fingers." Children immediately make associations; it's a universal language.

Dance can be used with children within the same class who cannot communicate verbally for a multitude of reasons, either because of a physical or emotional handicap or because of a foreign language. I don't need to speak the language of a child to understand what that child is trying to say to me. A child can simply toss his head to one side or the other, or lift her hand a little bit behind her back or head, and I know he or she is slightly uncomfortable with what's going on. To the teacher, body language is very important. The more that I communicate through the language of the body, as opposed to the word, the more it will help the child communicate to me through the body.

I have a fabulous opportunity to show the children how each of them is capable of and responsible for looking into any particular image and coming up with his or her own feeling. I realize that each of those children will come up with a different image, a different dance; and they will be attracted to different movements to accompany that dance. They'll be lured by a certain poem that will help describe that feeling. But they'll look at each other and realize that, in reality, they were all inspired by a single image like a shell from the ocean; yet the dances that they finally say, or speak, or move, will be very, very different. And yet, each one is valid.

That validity is extremely important because, generally, we have right and wrong, black and white. This is one way of helping the children realize that there's a very large spectrum of possibility. I think most children instinctively have that; but there's the fear of letting it out, fear of being wrong. We're so educated for right and wrong.

Once we get to the point where the children trust their own imagination and trust that within them they have their own substantial vocabulary to speak through movement, then comes the lovely area where we start focusing, harnessing that energy towards something specific that we want to say.

Children have a tremendous sense of imagination. Given a safe environment in which to play with that imagination, they're simply amazing; they're very deep. It's not so much that they become inhibited with age. Rather, they become more inhibited as they hear from the world around them that certain things are not right. A child learns that if a is the problem, then b is the answer. Often the children do not learn that if a is the problem, b, c, d, e, and anything else they might come up with may possibly be a solution.

Children, as they grow older, learn that there is an answer rather than that there is the possibility of an answer. They should be learning that there is a process by which we come to a solution—rather than this is the answer, there are no two ways about it. That's the sadness. We're not talking about an imagination run rampant, but rather an attempt to encourage the imagination and validate what children see. Through this digging into themselves, they really learn to become disciplined; they learn that they need to sensitize themselves, to dig deeper, and that it's work. They realize they have a tremendous sense of freedom that they can express. They can see something, and they can have opinions; it doesn't have to be wrong or right.

I've always had a curiosity for why things are as they are. Why does one person see something one way and another see it in a different way? And I've been curious as to how communication takes place. I've always felt that deep, deep communication could happen even though perhaps one couldn't speak. When I was younger, I worked as a volunteer in Bolivia in orphanages where there were deaf and mute children. That was the beginning for me of a realization that in silence there is a language. With those children, the whole issue was silence. I began choreographing in silence, trying to find the bridge of communication. Of course, it was in the gesture and facial expression.

I've also worked with children with *given circumstances*, a phrase I feel is the appropriate way of describing handicaps or disabilities. One episode that is especially memorable to me was a situation with a child in a wheelchair, a person no different from anyone else. When we divided into groups, she joined one group. The children were working on an image of a volcano. Given everyone's ability and disability— physical, emotional, shyness, etc.—each child presented part of the image. The child in the wheelchair was the beginning of the volcano; she was the rumbling, the shaking, even using the wheelchair for effect. Very beautiful! She is a child, a human being, capable of communicating. It's the other children who need to understand that.

Everyone has a different way of perceiving, and everybody on this earth has a right to perceive as they choose.

Bob Blue is a second grade teacher, songwriter, and singer in Wellesley, Massachusetts. His songs have been sung by other performers around the country and the world. He has recorded one album, "Erica Levine and Friends." He is the father of three children and stepfather of two.

Bob Blue: It's really important for music to be fun. The songs selected for use with preschool children should be so much fun to sing that it's okay that there's a message in there. The music has to be really appealing to children. Some people do it through rock music. A lot of very young children look up to their older brothers and sisters and adopt their pace, so sometimes it will be really loud electric guitar music. It should be something that children get really excited about, so that whatever message is in the song, whatever we're trying to communicate through the music, fits into the way they want to go about doing things.

They have to hear the message, though. They have to hear that the song really is making fun of something negative or saying something important. And usually they do, although sometimes it's almost as though we're putting words in their mouths, which isn't a good thing to do. But other kinds of words are put in their mouths as they're growing

up, so it's nice that they hear another point of view, even if sometimes
it's kind of heavy-handed.

For example, I took an issue that should be important to us, an issue that
we want children to be ready for, but talked about it on their level. I
wrote a song about exclusion. A girl in my class felt excluded from a
friendship, and I wrote a song about it. She's White, and the two friends
who are excluding her are White; but she knows what it's like to be
excluded. The song is not about apartheid; it's about this little girl
whose best friend deserted her and is now excluding her. It's the same

Photograph by Subjects and Predicates

message—it's unfair, it hurts—but it's right on her level. It's talking to her about what she's feeling. And later she'll grow up; and when she hears about injustice, maybe she'll think about the time that her friends excluded her.

The song needs to be simple enough, repetitive enough so that children can sing it; or, if it's not easy to learn but it's interesting enough, they'll try extra hard to learn it. It can be a tune that gets their bodies moving or sometimes just has intriguing intervals between notes. I don't concentrate too much on tunes when I write songs; I think about the words. But, in fact, the songs that seem to work for children are songs that have just the right amount of challenge in learning to sing them. Maybe it is an octave they have to sing, so their voices slide up; they love sliding their voices up to the top note they have to reach.

However, they also like knowing what's going to come next. If there are lots of verses, they like to have choruses that they can lean back on. They get really quiet during the verses because they're not sure of the words; but they know that the chorus is coming up, and they will be able to blast out the chorus. They also like learning songs in other languages because they like doing stuff that they know is hard to do and that they can do well. In the car, on the way home, they can sing a song in another language and impress their families.

One way to deal with cultural differences is to bring in music from around the world. Just the tunes from around the world give children a sense of other cultures. Learning to sing songs in other languages and what those songs mean expands their awareness of the world. Avoid songs that make only adults feel good. Some songs are ones that adults love to hear children sing because it makes adults think, "Boy, I'm really getting these kids to be idealistic." I've walked by classrooms where children are singing these songs; the children are not glowing, but the teacher is sitting there glowing. They're Mickey Mouse songs, and the children can't really sink their teeth into them.

Learning songs in other languages is one thing I do with my classes. Another is writing songs, both by myself and with children, that get them to think beyond themselves. Working with children is fun. I love singing with children; I love children's voices and their enthusiasm about singing. The reason I became a teacher and not a musician is that I wanted to make a big difference in the world. Something I learned a long time ago taught me that music is a diversion, music is not the way to make a big difference in the world. I'm not sure that's true. But so far, I feel as if teaching is the way to make a difference, and music is one of many media I use. It feels as if I'm doing something important. I'm trying to create a peaceful world, and singing with children and teaching children is my way of contributing.

Richard Lewis is an author, editor of numerous anthologies of poetry (including **Miracles: Poems by Children of the English-Speaking World** *and* **In a Spring Garden***), and founder and director of the Touchstone Center for Children in New York City.*

Richard Lewis: My work with children began with a class in literature in an art center in New Jersey. What was so exciting to me, from the first, was to reach into the imaginative lives of children and to realize the extent of their imaginations. So much of their imaginative lives seemed to be untapped and unchanneled. That moved me deeply—opening up the imagination as something integral to all human thought. That was and still is the motivating force of much of what I do—releasing and revealing to children the imagination and helping them give it shape and form.

Poetry is often a way of saying something we can't say in any other way. The beauty of all forms of art, whether it be poetry or painting or dance, is that it really is an alternative way of speaking about something that we find difficult to speak about through ordinary speech. And because art is often metaphoric in nature, it allows us to make our understanding of something clearer through creating the particular kind of imagery found in a poem, a story, or a dance.

With very young children, I work improvisationally, making up stories and poems with them. Often these stories or poems are based on experiences or images the children might initiate or on themes that I suggest that have universal appeal to be of interest to all of us. For example, I might begin this improvisatory process by cupping my hand in such a way that it looks like a bird. As I speak about the bird who flew through the room, happy to see the sunlight again, I might ask the children to tell me what they feel like when they wake up in the morning.

As each child responds, what begins to emerge is a group, as well as an individual, expression of waking up. I might copy these verbal expressions onto a piece of paper in order to make a story or poem; or I might have each child, just as I did with the bird, show me through gesture and drama how he or she reacts to the morning. I might, if time permits, paint a large mural with the children, depicting a portrait of themselves waking up, accompanied by their verbal expressions written out on the mural itself.

Sometimes with young children I use poems from different cultures as a way of speaking about how particular persons feel about a natural phenomenon—for example, how the Eskimos feel about snow or the Navajos feel about the dawn. The important thing is the feeling and how each of us can express a personal feeling towards anything we experience and know. The poems we read to children should act as a catalyst for their feelings and perceptions; and much of this happens when they not only identify with the imagery of the poem, but with the person reading and sharing the poem as well. If the person is sensitive to the imagery within the children themselves and can help the children bring out what they are feeling, then using poetry with young children can be an inspired sharing.

My advice to teachers of young children would be to listen carefully to children as they speak with each other and with us. In their conversations, children play, in effect, with so many different ideas, thoughts, and feelings. Our role is to help children use their language, their way of speaking, so that first of all, they respect it themselves. If children feel comfortable with how they express what is important to them, then their natural use of poetic and mythic language will begin to emerge. If they see that there are poems and stories by persons from cultures throughout the world that are about ideas and feelings similar to their own thinking and experiencing, then literature, not as a literary artifact but as a living and breathing expression, will make sense to them.

Susan Epeneter and Candace Chang are consulting editors with Exchange Press Inc.

Chapter Three
Staffing with Diversity

"There's no substitute for personal contact with people who are 'different' to help children realize they aren't really very different at all." Danny Deardorff in **Seattle's Child,** November 1986.

Honoring Diversity: Problems and Possibilities for Staff and Organization

by Margie Carter

In the early childhood field, we have a number of ways of referring to our work with differences: mainstreaming, multicultural, family groupings—to name a few. These describe our efforts to honor the needs of individual children and to recognize the pluralistic society in which we live. Many programs have chosen to specialize in one of these focused needs, while others try to incorporate programming for different needs into their general structure.

Most early childhood centers want their programs to represent at least a taste of living in a pluralistic society. Some very intentionally set out to have their programs counteract our society's institutionalized discrimination based on differences, especially as this relates to race, culture, and sex role biases. In each case, programs that want to accommodate differences among the children and families they serve must be clear about their goals, and they must have a responsive organizational structure.

I became acutely conscious of this when I was hired as the director of a child care program that did not have such clarity or strength in its organizational structure. It wasn't a bad program, but there was no clear vision driving it towards a set of goals or inspiring the staff or parents to come together with a sense of purpose. I found myself asking, "What if seeking, honoring, and learning from diversity became the guiding principle for all decisionmaking and structuring of our center's program? How would our environment and curriculum look? What would change in our enrollment, finance, and personnel policies? Where would I begin in making the necessary changes?"

What do we believe about diversity?

It took a period of trial and error before I realized that my first task was to create a clear philosophical statement regarding the concept of diversity. To develop a motivating vision, the staff had to come together to state what we believed and what we wanted to create. To build some common understanding and agreements about the value of diversity, we used our staff meetings to reflect on our experiences and knowledge. Over the years we deepened our insights and came to discuss them along the following lines:

We live in a society in which differences are usually avoided if not feared. Why is this? Often, quite unconsciously, we have absorbed concepts of *normal* and *abnormal, friends* and *enemies* developed by those with the resources to shape popular culture. Through them we come to see human qualities as split into superior and inferior, righteous and evil, loser and winner. This, in turn, shapes our self-esteem, our sense of security, and our behavior when we encounter the unfamiliar.

We tend to think in terms of the good guys and the bad guys. Psychologists tell us that the creation of enemies is often based on denied self-hatred. This notion and the understanding that our country was built on racism and attitudes such as *might makes right* and *the best and the brightest* can inform our insights into human development. Our challenge as early childhood educators is to counter these influences with a program that offers a different view and experiences from which to learn. Our goal is to develop the understanding that our security and our strength as individuals comes from our interconnectedness with others. We want children to learn that all forms of life are precious and to believe that they will benefit greatly from the presence of those different from themselves.

We know that the understanding of *strength through diversity* came long before modern economists, humanists, or civil rights advocates. In his scientific research, Darwin discovered that an environment tends to be richer and more sustaining to all the life in its boundaries when many different varieties of life forms exist within that environment. What an important understanding to bring to our early childhood programs!

As we come to understand that there are truths we do not see when we use only one kind of eyes, we will seek out someone different than ourselves. Conceptually, our goal of working with differences must embrace more than a strategy for civil rights or fair representation. It is a matter of expanding our humanity and having a vision of the potential for collective growth that diversity offers.

What makes diversity work for and not against us?

Getting clear about our beliefs is an important step, but only the first of many, in honoring diversity in our early childhood programs. We need clear goals that will guide administrative policies and program and staff development. Ideal as it may seem, one program cannot include the full range of differences possible within the human family—age, sex, race, culture, religion, physical and mental abilities. The type of differences that we incorporate into our programs must be limited to those that will enable us to remain strong and cohesive and to prevent fragmentation and divisiveness.

One of the lessons I quickly learned in my center was that, although programs with diversity can be a tremendous source of strength, they are also rich in conflict. Developing guidelines for learning from our dissimilarities and creating equitable policies to address our differences are essential ingredients to making the whole idea work.

What personnel policies strengthen diversity?

If diversity is a program priority, it will immediately be visible among the staff. This is our greatest challenge, given today's staff shortages and poverty level wages. It is a formidable task to not only find but also to keep desirable teachers. When a diverse group of people come together to consciously influence the next generation, the personal and professional growth available to them is enormous. To a certain extent this can offset the negative aspects of the salary and stress. The task then is to translate this motivational factor into an effective staff recruitment program. A polished marketing package may help in this effort, but the primary recruitment will come from those staff members who enthusiastically and regularly tell others outside the program about their work and growth.

Recruitment. A program that serves multi-ethnic families is usually conscientious in seeking a diverse staff in order to provide role models for the children. If the program population is primarily homogeneous, it is even more important that we diversity our staff so as not to further a misrepresentation of the world in our learning environments. Staff hiring can be approached with an informal needs assessment or a rigorous affirmative action plan.

Gentle Dragon Child Care Center in Seattle, Washington, has chosen the latter approach. For their overall program their policy is to have a staff that is 60 percent people of color and 40 percent White. Within each classroom, they strive for a staff balance of at least one male, one Spanish-speaking person, and one who knows sign language. Through the Foster Grandparent Program, they also ensure that there is a grandparent for each class. To parallel their enrollment policies, Gentle Dragon also seeks to have at least 20 percent of their staff represent alternative family structures.

ollowing similar guidelines, Thorndike Street School in Cambridge, lassachusetts, has developed a plan they call *affirmative outreach*. Vhen a staff vacancy occurs, they send a job description and flyer nnouncing the opening to community agencies that represent the diverse opulations they seek. The mailing is followed by phone calls. If ecessary, they place ads on radio stations and in publications that target hese same populations.

Employment criteria. In hiring staff, I have discovered that I bring nconscious assumptions about age, economic circumstances, family, or ultural backgrounds to interview arrangements and questions. If I aven't thought through how these factors influence a candidate, I may nintentionally discriminate against the very person who would be an sset to the program. Is English literacy a high priority for this staff osition? If not, the written application shouldn't be given too much veight. Am I seeking a grandparent figure to complement my staff? My nterview questions then need to focus on the experiences of the candidate, rather than her or his career path—"What has been most difficult or you in being with three year olds?" rather than "What do you hope to e doing five years from now?" If I am open to or seeking a single parent or the staff, I shouldn't schedule the interview at a time which complicates child care arrangements. When people with physical or mental disabilities are to be included on the staff, interviewing arrangements need to be suited to those circumstances.

Personnel policies. Personnel policies that address differing life circumstances will serve to attract a diverse staff. There is a delicate balance to be struck between the needs of the program and the group as a whole and then those of the individuals. Again, the policies of the Gentle Dragon and Thorndike Street programs can provide helpful examples.

Gentle Dragon Child Care established its program as a worker owned and managed collective. Recognizing that education, training, and experience are often the result of race, gender, and economic privilege in our unjust society, they decided to make the base pay for all staff equal. Additional salary, benefits, and all work arrangements are then offered according to need, rather than qualifications of education, experience, or seniority. Wage increments are offered for dependent children or parents. A health allowance is available for those whose health care needs cannot be met through traditional insurance policies. Parental leaves are available for women and men and adoptive parents. Child care fees are reduced to one third for staff members. Floating paid holidays have been included in their policies to allow for religious and cultural differences. In-service training for staff members includes management skills—a tremendous opportunity for those who might never have envisioned this for themselves.

The Thorndike Street School began offering an equal hourly wage for all; but they discovered that as staff gained experience and training, they moved on to higher paying jobs for which they were then qualified. In an effort to retain their staff, they changed the salary structure to include entry level and seniority wage differences and established assistant teacher positions for new teachers. This enabled their program to offer job mobility and a training base for those entering the early childhood education field for the first time or those moving from family day care homes to child care centers. The creativity both of these programs have brought to their personnel policies has made them attractive to diverse populations.

How do we build cohesiveness in the midst of diversity?

As diversity on a staff increases, so do the possible problem areas. Continual work must be done to build group consensus and a team spirit. We must take care not to assume everyone sees things in the same way, and we must take time to discover, appreciate, and learn from our differences. In doing so, we will recognize that both family backgrounds and cultural beliefs and practices influence the assumptions and behaviors we have acquired.

Photograph by Michael Siluk

In her new book, **Teaching Adults: An Active Learning Approach** (Washington, DC: NAEYC, 1986), Elizabeth Jones discusses methods she has used to help teachers become aware of what influences their own development, in order to better understand their work in the child development field. She asks people to look over a list of characteristics used to describe an *ideal child*. First they are to check the characteristics that indicate the kind of person their parents wanted them to become and to cross off those characteristics considered undesirable and usually discouraged or punished. They then repeat the process indicating the kind of person they would like their child to become. This exercise provokes passionate discussion and deeper insights into oneself and one's co-workers.

On other occasions, Jones has concluded a brief lecture introducing the concept of culture by asking those in the group who can confidently name their culture to stand up and do so. The rest of the group then joins those standing, forming small cluster groups to identify the different beliefs and behaviors of each culture named. This exercise helps teachers to distinguish fact from fiction in cultural stereotypes and also to uncover the discrepancies that occur between beliefs and behaviors. Incorporating such activities into our staff meetings will help us get to know ourselves and each other better. We may also clarify changes we want to make to overcome any acquired biases or behaviors that we don't want to pass along to the children in our care.

Regular staff meetings are essential for communications and decision-making in diverse groups. Without them, routine concerns can become a major source of tension. I remember well a center discussion on whether to have a policy requiring the children to eat all their food before leaving the table. One teacher said, "My family always used the line about the poor starving Chinese and I hated it." Another added, "We were never forced to eat anything in my family, and I think that has limited my acquired tastes." Almost under her breath a third voice said, "We just hoped there was enough food on the table when I was growing up." Almost by accident this staff discussion uncovered these dramatically different experiences influencing our views. It deepened our understanding and appreciation of each other and drew us closer together as a staff. From there we were able to more objectively discuss what message we wanted to convey to the children and to set our policy accordingly.

On another occasion the staff took up the question of what the center should do for Halloween. One teacher explained that the more she was reading about the historic role of witches as midwives, healers, and mediators in primitive cultures, the more uncomfortable she felt with the Halloween stereotype of witches as wicked and evil. "It's like blaming the victim. These women were burned at the stake by the thousands for their beliefs and practices." Another teacher spoke up, "In my church we are told not to celebrate Halloween because it is a pagan practice based on demons and sin. I've always hated it for that reason." Because the goal of the discussion was to explore and understand, the thinking of each of us was broadened by hearing these differing views. We created a Halloween party around the lesson that it is not only fun, but instructive, to pretend to be someone you really aren't—learning what life is like behind that mask.

Each of these examples could have been occasions for staff conflicts, divisions, and tensions; but instead we used them to bring us closer together across our differences. This happened not only because of the value we placed on diversity, but the concrete way we provided for staff discussions, using active listening and problem solving practices.

Things, of course, do no always go this smoothly. With the demands and stresses of child care work, staff tensions can mount to an intense level. To prevent things from deteriorating into personality conflicts or duplicities, we need a reference point against which we can test our assumptions and standards regarding acceptable staff behaviors. Such standards, along with a statement of how conflicts will be handled, should be included in written personnel policies if not staff contracts.

Ideally, these expectations and approaches to conflict resolution will parallel what we have set out for the children in our program. For instance, a statement might read: "At our center we all share in caring for each other and for the environment. When someone forgets or breaks this agreement, we remind them of how it hurts the group, explore why this happened, and work together to help the person get back on track. We work out disagreements by taking turns listening carefully to each other, explaining what we understand, and exploring what changes are possible and acceptable to those involved."

Over the years our staff developed a paper called "Staff Agreements and Approaches to Criticism When Agreements Are Broken" (see box). These agreements proved invaluable in helping us prevent unproductive criticisms based on subjective opinions or preferences. The investigative aspect countered the human tendency to become judgmental or defensive during a conflict.

What do our programs teach children about diversity?

Adult modeling accounts for a good part of what is significant for the children in our programs. The effectiveness of the environments we create for them, the materials provided, and the curriculum we design is dependent on our interactions with the children and with each other.

Much has been written about the importance of a multicultural curriculum in early childhood programs. What is important to emphasize here is that our curriculum approaches should indicate that there are many ways of seeing and living in the world, rather than conveying the message that the White Western view is *normal* and these others are exotic, supplemental, different, but not normal.

This means that rather than teaching a special lesson about Japan, we should include chopsticks, bowls, Japanese food packages, kimonos, tatami mats, and pagodas in our housekeeping areas or units about food, clothing, and shelter. Pictures around the room, fabrics, dolls, puzzles, and other learning materials should reflect diversity. When we teach about transportation we can include methods of transport that are used in a variety of cultures.

This approach is especially important for programs with a fairly homogeneous population. Children often respond to the unfamiliar with fear or rejection. Our task is to help them see differences as normal, familiar, acceptable, and useful.

The language we use is a crucial factor in how children come to view differences. While we want to teach them names for things, we want to avoid labels that reinforce stereotypes the predominant culture is conveying. Labels often confine understandings and thus acceptance. It is good to first describe what is being referred to before labeling it. "Taiko's eyes are brown, and they are shaped like this. That's one of the ways you can know she comes from an Asian culture" or "Jack's ears have trouble hearing. We call that being deaf." We don't want to convey that there is something wrong with a child who is the only one with certain characteristics. This not only isolates and defeats self-esteem for the child who is different, but for the other children it creates the impression that their characteristics are more acceptable.

References to families is another area where we must take care with our assumptions and language. Before the current prevalence of single parent families, many teachers automatically referred to families as mommy and daddy. We now recognize how that isolates the child who lives with only one parent and conveys the sense that this is not normal.

Less statistically visible, there are children in our program who are being parented by a grandparent or aunt, who live with foster parents or gay parents or a large extended family with many taking a parenting role. Our discussions of family life need to convey plurality and inclusiveness rather than pity, shame, or shock. Explorative discussions in staff meetings can enhance thinking and planning for the differences that exist in family structures and circumstances.

Does diversity come first in our enrollment practices?

Both Gentle Dragon and the Thorndike Street School make *intake choices* from the children on their waiting lists. Because of their commitment to diversity, they follow many of the same *affirmative outreach* approaches to enrollment that are used with staff recruitment. Quotas are set for certain populations, and spaces are reserved for them. Fees are determined in a similar manner, allowing for a variety of economic circumstances. All of this can be quite tedious at times if not financially risky. "Sometimes we get quite scared that we won't make our budget," exclaims a Gentle Dragon collective member. "But if we hold firm, the rewards are really worth it. One of our primary goals is to offer a multicultural learning experience to children of a variety of backgrounds and beliefs. Thus, cultural diversity is our highest priority in enrollment."

Where will it all lead?

Certain ideas and experiences have the power to transform our lives. If learning and growing from differences is a goal for the adults, and if they have an organizational structure responsive to that goal, it will be achieved for the children as well. Who knows where this might all lead? Perhaps it will be powerful enough to help in the transformation of our country as a whole. I'm a believer. Are you?

Margie Carter is the training coordinator at the Child and Family Resource Center in Seattle, Washington. This article is written in memory of Lenora Banks, a child care teacher who contributed greatly to Margie's commitment to diversity in early childhood programs.

Staff Agreements and Approaches to Criticism When Agreements Are Broken

1. We will each have an attitude of flexibility and cooperation in our work here, thinking of the needs of others and the group as a whole, along with our own needs.

2. We will each carry a full share of the workload, which includes some extra hours outside our work schedule (i.e. parent-teacher conferences, meetings, planning and preparation of activities, recordkeeping, progress reports).

3. We will each communicate directly and honestly with each other. We will be respectful and honorable in our interactions.

4. When problems or difficulties related to our work arise, we will address them rather than ignore or avoid them.

5. We will all be informed on significant problems that affect the center. These will be communicated in person as soon as possible and in writing as necessary.

6. We understand that it is appropriate to seek help from the director on sensitive or difficult issues.

7. When necessary, we will use a criticism/self-criticism discussion process to identify attitudes and behaviors that are negatively affecting our agreements.

Criticism/Self-Criticism Process—
to investigate and educate so we continue to adhere to our agreements.

Questions to ask oneself before giving a criticism:

1. Is my criticism based on investigation or on assumption?

2. What is the most important element of the criticism? Secondary?

3. What is my side of the problem, my responsibility or contribution to it?

4. What are my disguises that keep me from being criticized?

5. Is my criticism to hurt or attack or is it to educate?

6. How are our agreements hurt or helped by what I am criticizing?

7. How can I play a concrete positive role in helping the other person change?

8. What changes do I need to make in myself?

Stating a criticism:

When you do. . . .
I feel. . . .
It hurts our agreements because. . . .
Therefore I want you to. . . .
In the future I will behave differently by. . . .

Investigative discussion of the criticism:

Why do you feel that way? What happened?
What other things were going on? (objective things happening; subjective impressions, feelings)
What is the main thing that needed to happen here?

Are You a Dad AND a Teacher? Fathering a Year Long Curriculum

by Cory Gann and Sharon Stine

As an administrator, I greeted a request by one of my teachers to bring a baby to work with a mixture of anticipation and doubt. I had had previous experiences that raised questions and concerns about the difficulties of being both teacher and parent in a program for young children. But I was excited about the new kinds of learning this situation would offer to preschool children. Because the teacher making this request was a father, I felt that this was a special opportunity for children to experience on a day-to-day basis their teacher as a nurturing daddy. Perhaps this would have an impact on young children's understandings of what men do. To implement a curriculum that was a natural interweaving of children's understandings of gender roles seemed worth the risk.

We began with careful planning, trying to predict what Cory's day might be like. Complexity was a major issue. We thrive when there is a healthy match between the complexity of our work and our ability to cope. When there isn't enough complexity, we get bored and search for something to add that spice. When there is too much complexity, we get overwhelmed. And the need for complexity varies with the individual. Basically, I wanted to lessen the complexity for Cory, knowing that Caitlin, his ten month old, would be adding enough! We decided that being half time would be a realistic teaching load.

Staff support was essential, so our second task was to develop clear descriptions of what Cory would do and what might be difficult for him. This was discussed with team teachers and finally written down as specific job descriptions to clarify it for everyone.

Two issues emerged for Cory. First, how would he feel in a setting where he was supposed to know how to raise children but would be constantly on view to staff, students, and parents? Second, would he be able to stick to the more limited job description (half time) and not be seduced into overextending himself? What follows is Cory's story, which describes his weaving a texture of fathering into the daily lives of 40 children, three and four years old, during a year together in a morning preschool program.

Get Set . . . Go

FLASHBACK—It's 7:53 and Caitlin and I are on our mark, get-set, go for *seat wars*. She braces, then arches her back with more strength than I imagined from a ten month old baby. Megan, her six year old sister, complains that her seat belt is wedged. This morning's buckling is complicated by Caitlin's bulky coat. She gets lost in it, and the buckles don't fit over the fiberfill. I finish a quick inventory: Megan's lunch box, Caitlin's diaper carrier, plastic bag, backpack, bottle, extra juice, blanket for Caitlin, my coffee, materials for an art project. Yes, I am actually teaching today! We roll out of the driveway, hot on the heels of the bottleneck traffic jam lined up at the freeway on-ramp.

Inching along, I reflect on what's going on: In 40 households scattered around the city, parents and their children are scampering around, putting their own unique finishing touches on post-breakfast rituals designed to get them up and out, moving in tandem towards one common destination—to deliver their preschoolers to the Pacific Oaks play yard to be nurtured by a group of trained educators which includes me. Megan's first grade teacher, Ms. Knudsen, is busily setting up the science center Megan will explore once Caitlin and I deliver her to the gate of her classroom. Then we will hightail it back to the freeway to get to our destination to get ready for those 40 preschoolers. So, as I see it, 40 families are beating their brains out to get to me, while I'm beating my brains out to get Megan to Ms. Knudsen; and Caitlin is scrunched in her car seat ready to embark on a day of nurturing by her part-time teacher, full-time daddy. Now that I've got that straight, I'm ready for the day.

Settling In

Caitlin and I arrived surreptitiously, easing up preschool stairs at a toddler's rate. Our entrance was often characterized by Caitlin's guarded gaze: "I think I'll just make myself invisible today!" Sensitive co-teachers neither chorused nor ignored our arrival but greeted us naturally as if nothing out of the ordinary was happening. This daddy with his baby was ready, so he thought, to serve the needs of these three and four year olds as well.

I was instantly impressed by the natural groupings. We settled on the periphery of an activity; and there they were, like mercury from a smashed thermometer regathering itself into a ball: Evan, Jessica, Marshall, Jonathan, Megan, Lucera—each told their daily story of what

Photograph by Subjects and Predicates

their baby does at home, or how they cried when they were ten months old, or some expostulation about the general nature of raising babies. "It's hard!" said Jessica. "My mom works all the time." Here was a discussion, a conversation (language arts), each child in his or her own turn, listening to me and the others. Here was a self-selected group, organically cast, convening (at least for a while on a daily basis), anticipating the morning's coming together. Most surprising to me was the self-generating nature of it, inspired at first by Caitlin's presence, but then taking on a life of its own. The kids were clearly here because they liked the conversation. We had a four year old colloquium going, and once in a while we (yes, even I) got annoyed at Caitlin's fussiness.

The programmed baby unit we tried as an extension of our official family group structure went much differently. Caitlin and I regularly visited each small group of children at 11:30. I did baby care. We ate together—this group of preschoolers, teachers, and ten month old—and then I changed the baby. Children would get turns holding pins and diapers, watching and commenting, initiating discussions of anatomy and sex roles. **What is a Boy and What is a Girl** (Stephanie Waxman, Culver City: Peace Press, 1976), a marvelous children's book, was propped ready on the bookcase; anatomically correct dolls were available for immediate dramatic play. The lesson we learned from all this preparation and planning derived not from Caitlin, or the children, but rather from the set of attribute blocks with which most of the kids busied themselves once eating was finished and Caitlin had inconsiderately nodded off. "Ah ha," I commented professorially to my teaching assistant, "One of the essential attributes of attribute blocks is that they don't take morning naps."

Where Is Her Mom?

I must confess to having the same thought a time or two myself when the whole of it just got to me. But important questions come in spurts and bits, the tender topic talk and the tenderly rigid views of pre-operational thinkers. "Is it a boy or a girl?" Evan asked daily, only the syntax of the question changing from time to time. "Is THAT baby a boy or a girl?" Evan greeted us one particular morning and I couldn't help correlating his emphatic tone with Caitlin's attire for the day—blue coveralls and a sweatshirt complemented by her standard *you go anywhere you want* baby hairstyle. "Where's her mom?" was Catherine's query, echoed several times a week by classmates trying to get used to the two of us.

When Caitlin fell or scraped herself, "Where's her mom?" got my more curt response. "At work!" I would say, holding Caitlin while she cried, hugged me tightly, and lapsed into recuperative quiet. As her playfulness returned, I conversed more freely with a few still concerned companions. "Her mother is a teacher just like me, only at a different school with older children. So I take care of Caitlin during the day." We all walked inside to get Caitlin's diaper changed. The kids held pins and set down the changing pad. Caitlin kicked her legs to make a better test of my competency with an audience. Task completed, Caitlin rolled herself into a crawling position just in time for Evan to ask once again, "Is your baby a boy or a girl?" I'm left to wonder about the preschooler's conservation of gender, at least when it comes to babies.

But Sometimes I Wonder

Caitlin's fussiness threshold was three minutes at the sandbox and four and a half minutes in the trike area. It did not occur to me that by bringing my baby with me to work I was also embarking on a regime of what could be called *teaching in motion* or, as one metaphorically inclined co-worker observed, "teaching as if you have to go to the bathroom all the time." Wonderful teaching moments were balanced by the limitations of my own baby's unpredictable demands when I had to move on. At the same time, one of the effects Caitlin had on me was to cause me to constantly think of her needs rather than the needs I had as a teacher. Leaving the sandbox or trike path so precipitously could also be described as your basic *leaving children in the lurch*. The antidote for me was a clear yell for help to other staff as we bounced our way out of the

Photograph courtesy of Pacific Oaks

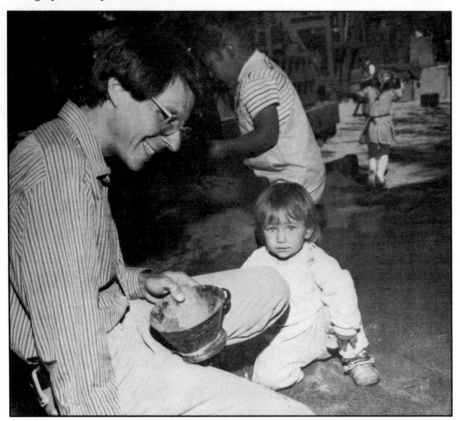

sandbox on to the next step of *roving and floating*, as it's known in the lexicon.

Caitlin's presence did have an impact on both the children and myself as we dealt with social problems. On more than one occasion, Caitlin stood squarely in between two momentary combatants, trustfully calibrating the escalation of emotion: "I had it first!" "No, I did!" "No, I did!"

Even amidst hotly agitated disputes, our three and four year olds tempered their ferocity in deference to Caitlin's petite innocence. Maybe she lent a measure of perspective to all those ego-tinged conflicts. The truth of the matter is that she emerged unscathed from one fray after another.

I did plunge in less often than I would without Caitlin, which worked to the behavioral objective of *letting kids work it out for themselves*. But I sometimes wonder! What do kids lose when we don't take that teacher step which has all the earmarks of just the *right move*? I remember a fairly complex play drama which was unfolding one morning in front of the climbing structure. London and Geoffrey were driving the large rectangular box, bedecked in yellow raincoats and fire fighter hats, obviously immersed in a fire engine scenario. What impressed me was the careful inclusion of useful and symbolic things which were fetched deliberately over a matter of minutes. London brought over one of the smaller ladders and hooked it along the side of the box. Geoffrey propped a sandbox shovel into the crate's handle groove, creating a convenient post for the coiled fire hose (15 foot jump rope). Even an adult could envision this hook and ladder, siren-blasting its way through the rush hour congestion of the preschool yard.

Sergio deftly attempted to become part of this game by sidestepping the normal social steps of entreaty and negotiation, assuming instead the cadence of this scene. He yelled "Fire!" at the top of his lungs and pointed to the upper deck of the climbing structure. Quickly, Geoffrey unravelled the rope/hose and leapt up in hot pursuit of the *burning embers*.

The teacher voice within me chimed in loudly about what my next move ought to be. *"Move that green garden hose sitting near the ramp closer to their truck. Be unassuming, and you don't need to say a word. See if the addition of the real hose anchors their play and facilitates the inclusion of Sergio."* The clarity of this message charged my nerve endings and practically mobilized the rest of me into action, only to ram full force into the gentle daddy of me sitting patiently on the porch steps, nestling my baby in my lap! The two of us were sharing the story unfolding before our eyes.

In a moment Geoffrey and London were off and away. Sergio was left lamenting the refrain, "They won't play with me. . . ."

What Did You Learn, Cory?

Just before the end of the school, Megan asked if she could skip one day of first grade in order to spend the morning with Caitlin and me. We chose the day, and Megan selected a favorite picture book to read to the four year olds during their group time. The influence of a six year old story reader held the kids spellbound for several pages. Gradually, the listeners drifted away to work on their end-of-the-year remembrance albums of photos and art work. As three or four children got started on the project, Megan forged ahead in her book with the remaining story hold-outs. Caitlin veritably pranced in a circle, pulling selective papers off the shelves and humming a made-up tune to herself as she had started to do those days.

As the memory books took form and shape, each child commenced the task of signing their cover page, each with his or her degree of legibility and competence, some already adding flourishing strokes, some omitting the tougher letters. Marshall offered an editorial comment in the middle of writing his name, "S is the difficult letter. I always used to mess it up." I responded, "It's amazing, Marshall. In September, you couldn't write any letters, and now here you are signing your name. And at the start of school, Megan didn't know how to read, and now here she is reading a story to the whole group. And not only did Caitlin learn how to walk, she is dancing around!" Lily dotted her *i* and admired her work a second; then she asked, "What did you learn, Cory?"

To answer Lily's question, I didn't really learn something new as much as I learned it better. In a way, Caitlin became everyone's sibling during the ten months, adding all the joys and headaches the arrival of a new baby sister brings. I remember being prone to an unusual cringe when loving children in my class would, uninvited, pick Caitlin up from behind, only to be on the receiving end of a well-decibeled squelch she developed for such occasions. Caitlin was a catalyst for the emerging sense of *other* which it is every preschooler's task to develop—another person, even so small, with other feelings, responses, expectations, and, of course, rights.

As a parent at work, the *other directedness* of Caitlin's presence was a humbling experience. With Caitlin I was having to think all the time about behaviors that caused me not to be a *good* teacher in the eyes of others. Here was somebody I cared about on a minute-to-minute basis even more than my job performance! A song not finished, an art activity never quite set up, a question where the answer trailed in the wake of my baby's more immediate need—these are recollections to chuckle about with Caitlin when one day we thumb through snapshots of our year together. For my class, these will hopefully not matter at all, or hardly as much as the experiencing of their teacher, a father and his baby.

Weaving It All Together

Bringing a baby to work is an individual decision but it impinges on many people who become the network of caring, understanding, and support. By trying something that none of us had done before, we knew the risk carried unknowns that would trip us up from time to time. When tensions resulted—"Cory is always holding that baby!"—staff talked out their frustrations. Babies make different demands; their needs must often come first. Not only was the teaching team working with this issue, the children were also learning when their teacher was needed by his baby. They became more aware of their teacher as a family member. He didn't live at school; he had a baby and a home with the baby's mother and sister. Their comments about families, particularly their own, were a window to a growing interest in figuring out about mothers, fathers, siblings, babies, and, ultimately, their place in these linkings of people.

Although teachers bucked up against new frustrations, one of the known factors that added stability to the program was that the staff had worked together before. They already had established a teaching relationship that included a willingness to talk about problems immediately, to share feelings, frustrations, and some delightful humor and playfulness.

Our early assessments of what Cory would be able to do and what would be difficult for him were very close to the mark. That initial thinking, writing, and clarifying of everyone's roles formed a foundation of needed predictions. Before our daily experiences began, we discussed the difficult reality that Cory might have to pull out if the program was not working for Caitlin (the plan's most unpredictable ingredient). Even though this didn't happen, looking at the issue early in our planning stages gave everyone a better understanding of some limits of this unknown venture.

Our story is not necessarily a model for other programs. Rather, it points out the need to develop an ongoing curriculum about sex differences that includes daily experiences with fathering models—experiences that are ongoing rather than occasional appendages. When we limit ourselves to a theme plan, such as a week of gender role activities, we run the risk of providing an exotic tour curriculum where being a nurturing male is the unusual, not the day-to-day way people live as loving human beings.

Sharon Stine is currently in private practice as a consultant with a group of early childhood professionals known as The Branch. The previous six years she was director of children's programs at Pacific Oaks College. Cory Gann is a master teacher in the preschool program at Pacific Oaks College and Children's School in Pasadena, California.

Chapter Four
Learning from Parents

"For adults, consciousness raising is often needed to move from a state of ignoring differences to one of identifying and joyfully exploring differences." Mary Lynn Porter, Auburn Day Care Centers, Auburn, Alabama

Tossed Salad Is Terrific: Values of Multicultural Programs for Children and Families

by Janet Brown McCracken

"Mom," four year old Erica asked as we climbed into the car to start the commute home, "are we juice?"

"Are we juice?" I repeated in a puzzled voice.

"Yes, are we juice?" she insisted. "All the juice kids pretended to be Moses and the people who got treated mean, but I had to watch."

It was then I recalled seeing a notice that a parent was going to make potato latkes with the children in Erica's child care center for Seder as part of Passover. She wanted to be Jewish, too, so she could be a part of the action!

All through her five and a half years in Broadcasters' Child Development Center in Washington, DC, we have had the privilege of knowing a variety of parents and teachers, in a supportive setting, who wanted the best for children—some are middle-income White, like us; many others are Black, Asian, and Spanish-speaking. The experiences all of us have shared, and the warm feelings about the potpourri of people we have come to admire, respect, and love will last a lifetime. This wealth of opportunities could never really be duplicated by a family without the advantages of a high quality child care program that instills in staff and families alike the value of individuals—a tossed salad approach—rather than a melting pot in which everyone is expected to conform to one set of expectations.

Knowing Real People

The good feelings about the value of this type of multicultural education are built around the small, everyday incidents in which children, parents, and teachers come to know each other as people. These experiences are far from trivial, because they are the reality of everyday life, shared with others. No artificial celebrations of holidays, books, or movies about other people, visits to museums, or any other secondary experiences could possibly have the impact that these valued human relationships—with parents, teachers, and children—have had in cementing a genuine respect for people. Let's look together at how such everyday contact with others forms the basis of a strong multicultural program for families.

Teresa Teyes, a toddler teacher, immigrated from Bolivia and has just become a U.S. citizen. She often speaks to the children in Spanish, so much of their first language has a Spanish inflection, and the early exposure to Spanish still appears occasionally in their speech. The value of this early exposure to the variety of language was evident on vacation in Canada when Erica was four. She quickly picked up the rhythm of the French she encountered and delighted in playing waitress, all in French. Erica still says "lellow" instead of "yellow," and adamantly denies that she speaks English. It may well be that this interest in languages, and the ability to hear and repeat various inflections, will serve these children well the rest of their lives.

Teresa's niece, Gigi, and Erica became the best of friends as toddlers. Four years later, they continue to greet each other with hugs and talk about each other frequently, although they rarely get together. The depth of the girls' friendship was demonstrated when Gigi's mother was about

Photograph by Subjects and Predicates

to remarry; Gigi was very resistant to the idea. Erica has been through a similar situation, so Teresa asked Erica if she could talk with Gigi about it. Erica enthusiastically told Gigi, "I was a grown up flower girl at Mom and Jim's wedding. And you know what? It's great to have two dads. Some people have two moms and some have two dads." Erica's support clearly helped Gigi feel more comfortable in dealing with her blended family.

Birthdays are another important time for families from different cultures to share. Erica has attended two of Gigi's birthday parties where she was one of the few English-speaking children. "We had a great time, Mom. When can I go back to Gigi's again to play with her and her friends? Her new dad was real nice, too."

Teresa's generosity, even on her abysmally inadequate teacher's salary, has led her to insist on making Erica's birthday cake for her party at school. The cake is a low-sugar one, her mother's specialty, and always beautifully decorated with the symbols most meaningful to Erica—for her fifth birthday the cake was graced with a beautiful rainbow.

Teresa's cheerful greetings every morning, and her genuine interest in every family in the center, have added immeasurably to the love and valuing of the diversity of wonderful people.

Another long-time staff member, Shirley Watkins, teaches the oldest group, and parents are always so pleased when their children finally reach Shirley's team—they have seen how wonderful she is! Shirley has that rare gift of natural respect for people of all ages. She exudes warmth and understanding, whether it is the parent or the child who is having a difficult time. As a Black parent with four children, she knows what to expect even in the most difficult of situations, and just how to listen and respond with soothing and comforting words.

The *Shirley stories* she tells about her own childhood clearly hold the children spellbound, because they can relate so well to her experiences. One powerful story that is a favorite of the children goes like this, according to Erica (complete with appropriate gestures and sound effects):

One night Shirley took a bath (washing motions). *She went upstairs and her Grandmother tucked* (tucking the covers in) *her into bed. She tricked her Grandmother and she thought she was asleep. Shirley tiptoed downstairs* (finger to the lips and spoken quietly) *and then opened the door. And then she played in her sandbox. And then her Grandmother went downstairs and locked the door because she didn't know Shirley wasn't in her bed. Then Shirley heard scratching noises* (fingers scraping faster and faster). (With much animation) *They got louder and louder and*

he was scared! She tried to get back into the house, but the door was
ocked and she couldn't get in. She knocked on the door (knocking) and
er Grandmother let her in. When her Grandmother picked her up
(hugging), Shirley peed all over and said to herself she would never do
hat again! Then she took another bath and then she went to bed."

Shirley's ability to help children figure out solutions to their own
problems is unparalleled. She demonstrates caring and respect when she
listens. Parents and children alike learn a great deal about how to relate
to people from Shirley.

There are many other people and experiences in a multicultural center,
such as Broadcasters' Child Development Center, that also are memorable. Bob, for instance, who was first a toddler and then a preschool
teacher, speaks not only English but also Spanish and Chinese. He was
delighted when two Chinese children, Paul and Stephanie, enrolled at the
center. During those years every child in their groups frequently found
their names (or symbols) written in Chinese. Erica still loves Chinese
food, thanks to the cooking experiences at the center and her close
friendships with Paul and Stephanie.

Bob left the center in the summer of 1985 to serve as a volunteer in war-
torn Nicaragua before beginning graduate work in bilingual education.
There were many anxious moments for parents, teachers, and children
alike while he was gone. While driving to the center each day, we heard
the news. Every time Nicaragua was mentioned, which was frequently,
Erica (and I) would get a worried look on her face and note anxiously,
'That's where Bob is!" His letters assured all of us that his work with
children there was going well; but more than a year after his return, the
word *Nicaragua* still elicits an amazed, "That's where Bob went!"

One child in the program, Liana, was adopted at the age of three from
Korea, where life had been excrutiatingly difficult for her. She spoke no
English, but all the children immediately welcomed her and made her feel
at home. Bob and Shirley did, too, of course; and it was their special
understanding that helped Liana pick up English and friends faster than
it seemed could be possible. This energy-filled, outgoing child soon
became a big sister, and left the program. That was nearly two years ago.
Erica still talks about seeing her arrive at the public school upstairs with
her baby sister. Never once has she mentioned the fact that Liana has a
large birthmark on her face—to her Liana is one of many close friends.

There are many other families and children, too, whom we have come to
know and love. Marge Kumaki's patience, with a four year old and a new
infant, is exceptional. How many of us admire her ability to be so calm as
she arrives every morning with diapers, lunches, clothes, and bottles in

hand. And yet she often reads a story with a small group of attentive
children at the end of a hectic day at work! Or Reggie Todd, the father
who so skillfully held his newborn son throughout the preschool parents'
meeting for his older daughter. By observing other parents and teachers,
all of us can learn so much from each other about what it takes to make
the world a great place for children.

Work times are yet another way in which the diverse skills and needs of
parents and staff can be recognized and met. Together families from
various backgrounds serve as board members, work on fundraisers, and
find ways to achieve our common goal: the best possible experiences for
young children from three months to five years in a full day program.

Without the context of a multicultural center, none of us would ever have
had the opportunity to feel so close to such a variety of interesting people.
Our children have grown up, from infancy, surrounded by people who are
proud of their ethnicity, and at times each child has expressed a desire to
be what the other children are. This is healthy, because they have not
learned to stereotype people based on a preconceived notion of them. The
children and families know—and admire—each other, because they know
and respect each other.

It was not until Erica was four that she gave any indication that she
noticed skin color, and then only in passing she inquired whether
someone "was black like Anthony." She has always accepted people just
as they are; and with such a firm foundation, she and her friends always
will.

The Future

The tossed salad approach to early childhood education has been a
marvelous complement to the lives of every person in the program. Many
of the families have talked about how we anticipate that these rich
opportunities will continue as our children enter elementary schools. We
all hope there are other cultures in these new settings that will enable us
to broaden our world view even further.

*Janet Brown McCracken, M.Ed., an early childhood education
writer and photographer, is director of Subjects and Predicates.
She is the mother of two young children and a former child care
teacher and program director. She edited* **Young Child** *for ten
years and has written and edited a number of brochures and
books for the National Association for the Education of Young
Children.*

Building Positive Images: Interracial Children and Their Families

by Francis Wardle

"Teacher, who's that lady?"

"Which lady, Johnny?"

"The lady who brings Maia every morning."

"Oh, that's her mother."

"Well, then who's the man—the one who takes her home?" continued Johnny, uncertainly, with confusion in his voice.

"That's her father," the teacher replied automatically.

"But they aren't the same. . . ."

"That's true," said the teacher, suddenly realizing Johnny's confusion and trying to quickly come up with an answer that would make sense.

Before she could respond, Johnny interjected, "But Maia's not black like her mother. Is she black; or is she white, like her daddy?"

Children of mixed racial and ethnic backgrounds are an ever increasing phenomena in early childhood programs. These children are products of parents who have gone outside conventional identity groups to marry. Because of more interaction between different people in social, work, and school settings, there are more and more marriages outside of conventionally held options. Blacks marry Whites, Hispanics Whites, Asians Blacks, and so on. Children from these unions have unique problems that must be addressed by early childhood programs.

These children add to the richness of the early childhood experience for all the children in the child care setting. But teachers and administra-

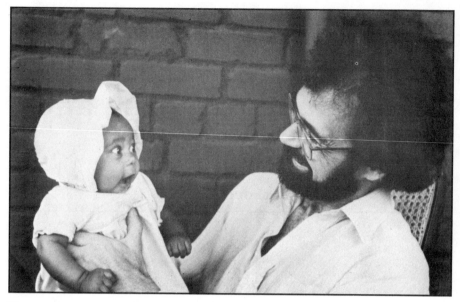

Photograph by Ruth Benjamin-Wardle

tors are often as confused as Johnny. Are these children Black, or are they White? Are they Hispanic? Are they Asian, or are they just American? Or, as Maia—a pretty, vivacious four year old with two little braids, an upturned nose, and sparkling eyes set in a round face—would have answered: "Mummy's black, daddy's white, and I'm brown."

I am Maia's father, an Englishman with black curly hair, brown eyes, and a proclivity for athletics and dance. Whenever people attribute Maia's hair, dark eyes, and balletic gymnastic skill to her Black mother, I get incensed. My four children have the strength of both cultures, and not necessarily according to stereotypical standards. Conventional thinking labeled any person with any Black heritage as being Black, any child of a White parent and one non-Black parent or parent of color as also being Black. While much of society still holds to these categories, and some parents of interracial children do, many parents of children of combined heritage subscribe to the idea that their children are products of both parents' heritages and their identity should reflect this clear heritage.

Terminology

"There are various viewpoints about the terminology to be used to describe children of interracial families: interracial, biracial, mixed, brown, and rainbow have all been suggested. The term interracial is used because it is inclusive of families with a variety of heritages: African, European, Asian, Native American, Hispanic, etc." (Shackford, 1984).

Support the Identity of Interracial Children

Professionals working with young interracial children must consider
three general directions in working with these children:

• Their own deep seated beliefs about this issue

Interracial relationships are contaminated by a history of racism and an
over analysis of the evils involved. Unfortunately, some professionals
working with young children are uneasy with this issue and believe all
mixed marriages are based on ulterior motives such as marrying for social
advancement or to protest society's racial prejudices. Staff should openly
explore this issue, maybe with a professional leader who can sort out the
feelings, attitudes, and prejudices.

• The views of the child's parents

Parents of interracial children set the tone for that child's identity. Many
of these parents will be struggling with the question at home and with
their relatives and friends. Ultimately, though, the program must
support the parents' views. A conference before school that explores the
issue of the child's identity is, therefore, a must. Talk to the parents
openly and non-judgmentally about the issue of their child's identity.
Suggest reading materials, support groups, and other interracial parents
in the program who might help the parents sort out their own feelings.

Don't force them to choose an identity for their child based on one
parent's identity or conventional societal categories. While the teacher
must support the parents' wishes on this issue, the teacher should also
assist the parents in exploring the entire question of identity. Many
interracial parents have not come to a definitive feeling on this issue.
They often feel isolated and believe they must use the conventional
identity categories. Let them know that other choices are available.

• The importance of a child's sense of identity to the child's overall development

How parents and teachers respond when children come to them with
questions is of great importance in shaping that child's self-image. "My
friend Mike is black, Gene is white. What am I?" "Jimmy (who is
Hispanic) says I'm black, and he isn't. But he's darker than me. Why?"
These questions were asked by Maia when she was four. We know young
children are very interested about themselves—their name, parents, hair,
size, age—and how they fit with other children. Teachers must be ever
aware and sensitive to each child's need to feel good about his/her physical appearance, physical and intellectual abilities, and family heritage.

But don't stereotype! "You're a good dancer like your mother (because she's Black)." "You have curly hair like your daddy (because he's Black)." "Your blue eyes are like your mummy (who is White)." Children want to know they are like their father and mother because they are their parents, not because all Blacks have curly hair, all Whites have blue eyes, all Asians are good at math!

Early Childhood Programs Must Support Interracial Families

All families of young children today are under extreme pressure: ever increasing cost of raising children; need for both parents to work; selecting and monitoring child care; anti-child mood in the country today; negative influence of television; one parent homes; fear of kidnapping and strangers; loss of anti-poverty programs. Interracial families have a particular kind of stress: new interracial families must struggle with the nation's rejection of the concepts and ideas that brought the family together.

In their daily lives parents of interracial children must face racism constantly; many have also lost the financial and practical support of parents and grandparents on both sides of the family. They often feel they are fighting a long battle against relatives who don't want them and a country that has gone back on its commitment to equality for all people.

The early childhood program can become a setting where much of this stress is alleviated, where interracial families can find new friends and helpers who will support them in their struggle, and who can tap into systems to fill the gap lost from relatives. Interracial couples are as serious as any other couple in raising healthy, well developed children. They should be helped and supported by the school in this effort. Parents of interracial children should feel the school is an active advocate and supporter of their desire to provide a good home and a good education for their children.

The early childhood program is one of the first settings where children must survive being different and come to grips with the often cruel world. Interracial children are, physically, so obviously different. This means the adult who is racially biased will pick on these children, and other children who are unusually curious about physical differences will pick on them. When a child is in an argument, he will find the first thing he can to make the other child seem inferior. If the other child is obviously interracial, that's what will be used. Other differences between children are less physically apparent and therefore are less likely to be used.

Early Childhood Programs Should Utilize the Richness of Interracial Children

Children of interracial heritage add a great deal to the richness and quality of the school setting. They bring at least two distinctive cultures; they have experience of dance, art, language, and culture richer than most children; and they have a broad base of knowledge. They play easily with children in the program from diverse backgrounds, and they bring an openness to the setting. Obviously, this richness and diversity will only be evident and an attribute to the program if it is recognized, encouraged, and supported.

Eirlys, my six year old, knows her heritage includes Black, English, American Indian, and Oriental. Thus, when her class studies the food, culture, dress, or geography of those areas, she has a personal interest

Photograph by Francis Wardle

and enthusiasm. She talks to her class about her English grandfather, her Black grandfather who still lives in Kansas City, and her Indian heritage. She is also enthusiastic about any different background and heritage. This openness to a cosmopolitan approach can be effectively used by teachers and picked up by other children. Most interracial children have a doubly rich heritage and life experience that can be an asset to the classroom. Other children will learn an enjoyment of people who look different and who have a different heritage.

Interracial children also resist the temptation for teachers and children to divide the child care experience into Black and White: Black and White dolls; Black and White pictures; Black and White fairy tales, histories, and festivals. They force the program to address the richness of all cultures that color the human existence; they encourage other children to realize that they cannot place all people into two either/or categories: Black and White, rich and poor, friend and enemy.

"Well, what are you anyway, Black or White?" asked the six year old of her schoolmate Maia.

"Actually, my daddy's English and my mummy's part Black and part Indian, and there's some Japanese in me somewhere. . . ."

"Oh, that's okay," interrupted the curious girl, "I'm sorry I asked."

This kind of interaction forces a child to think about racial categories, about placing other children into neat little boxes. When Eirlys did a picture of her family, she cut and pasted a Black woman for her mother, a White man for her father, two light skinned Blacks for her sister and brother (there are very few biracial models), then drew a baby with a brown crayon because she could find no photos of babies like her own. In a program that understands and appreciates the richness of people's heritages, and the dangers of placing people into cultural and racial stereotypical categories, efforts like this by interracial children add tremendously to the richness and cosmopolitan approach of the curriculum.

And what happens to the stereotypes? Interracial children, like other children, can be intelligent, beautiful, athletic, gifted; they can enjoy music and dance. (Mine are all of the above!)

From my experience knowing many interracial families, many of these parents are very concerned about their children's upbringing. They know they have challenged conventional attitudes, and they want to make sure their children will not suffer. They have thought a great deal about how they want to raise their children. So they are often active parents who become involved in their children's education and child care programs.

They will work to keep a program sensitive to their needs and their children's needs and demand that teachers reflect their feelings and attitudes toward their interracial children. A strong program that supports children and families of mixed racial and ethnic backgrounds will send a clear message to prospective parents about the program's policies.

Specific Ideas for Teachers

In working with these families, teachers and administrators must understand that interracial families are as different from each other as are any other families. They cover the whole range of economic, religious, educational, and value differences. Their children are as different as any other children from different homes. They cannot be stereotyped.

Teachers must be sensitive to children as individual personalities made up of varied and rich backgrounds. But even as they are aware of the multiheritage of a child's background, they must be watchful of the traps. *Recently my three year old, Kealan, and I were watching the world cup soccer games. He kept asking, "Who's the black man?" I noticed one of the teams was from Morocco, so I said, "The Black men play for an African team. Some people from Africa are Black." He was not satisfied and kept asking. Finally, he pointed to the television, asking, "That black man?" He was pointing to the referee who was dressed in black!* While it's critical to understand the child's interracial heritage and to be sensitive to his use of it in daily activities within the classroom, remember that the majority of his experiences will be like those of any other child—with little apparent reference to his interracial heritage.

• Meet with the parent(s) before each school year and regularly during the year. During these meetings discuss, along with issues that affect all parents and children, how the parents deal with their children's heritage and how they want the school to support it. How do they respond to racist remarks to their children? What do they say to their children?

• Include in the curriculum people of mixed racial and ethnic backgrounds. This should include children's books (see "Reflecting Diversity—Books to Read with Young Children" in this book) and pictures of biracial children and interracial couples, historical people of mixed racial and ethnic backgrounds, and current interracial heroes.

• While studying people, cultures, art, and dance, avoid breaking the world into racial groupings. Stress individuals; focus on how art, music, and dance transcend national, geographic, and racial boundaries.

• Allow for open and supportive questions about race, color, hair texture, heritage, and identity. Just as a four year old will ask, "Am I older than you?" and "Who's biggest?," they will ask, "Are you Black?" "Is your mother Mexican?" and "Am I darker than you?" When these discussions come up, remember what the child's parent has said about the child's identity and respond in terms of everyone having a rich heritage (Italian, German, Native American, Chinese, African, etc.). Remember that children are naturally very curious and don't want a deep explanation for what they see as simple physical characteristics. Obviously, the teacher must be comfortable with these discussions.

• Allow children of different racial and ethnic backgrounds to play in the housekeeping corner as married couples. If other children comment, use this as an opportunity to talk about the naturalness of different people—national, religious, and racial—marrying. Be positive.

• Help biracial and multi-ethnic children to feel proud of their heritage. Help them to identify other biracial and multi-ethnic children in the program, or a biracial staff person, or biracial people in pictures or materials in the classroom. Help them draw people like themselves, use dolls that are like them, and encourage them to impose their physical features into pretend play and art activities. Don't try to avoid the issue.

• Utilize interracial children's experiences and heritage to expand activities for all the children. Discussion on interracial heritage can include national heritage of all children, religious combinations, and interesting physical attributes: "Where did you get your green eyes and red hair?" "Was your grandfather so tall?"

Have children bring in pictures of their relatives. Discuss the countries children came from, the languages and customs. Have parents and grandparents visit the program and talk about their lives. Use children whose parents are different to discuss differences, how all children respond to them, how differences should not be feared, how learning about differences can be fun.

• Help these children stand up to children and adults who attack their identity. Help them protect themselves and retain their pride.

• Help these children to understand that some people see them as different, that it's okay to be different, that many of the great people of the world are proud to be different.

• Try to expose these children to role models. Invite interracial couples to your program; encourage a variety of teachers and volunteers; mix older multiracial and multi-ethnic children with younger children.

• Understand that most of these children's problems and their parents' problems have nothing to do with their mixed heritage. It is too simple to scribe problems to their unique heritage, and it will encourage these children to use their background as an excuse.

• A child's positive identity at this age is directly tied to how he feels about his physical characteristics, how he feels about his family and his friends, and what he can do (art, music, reading, climbing, etc.). So the most important thing the program and its staff can do is to make the interracial child and his family totally accepted in the program. The child must feel positive about his physical features; the parent(s) must feel accepted and supported when they visit; the child must feel good about a particular accomplishment because *he* did it.

Interracial children and their families provide a rich contribution to early childhood programs. They bring a multiplicity of experiences, knowledge, and exposure to the program. These additions should be effectively utilized by program staff to enhance learning for other children, to support the richness of diversity and difference, and to enrich the entire curriculum. The program should also utilize interracial parents' efforts and interest in their children's development to strengthen the program.

References

Aldridge, D. "Interracial Marriage: Empirical and Theoretical Consequences," **Journal of Black Studies**, 8 (3), 1978, 355-368.

Baptiste, P. "The Contemporary Interracial Child," **Communique**, April 1985, 1-7.

Baptiste, P. "Rearing the Interracial Child," **Communique**, December 1983, 4-5.

Interracial Books for Children Bulletin. "Children of Interracial Families," 15 (6), 1984.

Shackford, K. "Interracial Children: Growing Up Healthy in an Unhealthy Society." **Interracial Books for Children Bulletin**, 15 (6), 1984, 4-6.

Wardle, F. "Mummy's Black, Daddy's White, and I'm Brown," **Communique**, Fall 1985, 4-7.

Wardle, F. "Please Check One—White, Black, Other, Mixed," **Communique**, September 1984, 2-3.

Francis Wardle, Ph.D., is the father of four interracial children, a writer and photographer, and director of Adams County Headstart in Denver, Colorado.

Parenting a Child with Special Needs

an interview with Meg Robinson

What is it like for the parents when their child has a disability?

When you have a child who has a disability, there's a lot that goes on. You go through the same stages you go through in any kind of very difficult situation. First, you have denial of the problem; every parent has denial in varying degrees. Then you want to hide it, make it a secret. No one should know that my child has a disability, that my child is going to be labeled. Then you have to try to deal with what the implications of the disability are for the child, for you as the parent of the child, for the school, and so on. And it's not like you go through all those adjustments and then wrap it up and put it on a shelf. The adjustment is an ongoing kind of thing—there are peaks and plateaus; you gradually reach some hurdles and you get over them.

I sound like I'm being very negative; I'm actually very positive. You gain a lot, too. It helps you become a more sensitive person, more aware of other people. I'm certainly more sensitive to anyone who has a disability as a result of having a child with that sort of problem. And the child develops subtly other strengths as a means of compensating for having the disability—and those can be very rewarding.

How can early childhood teachers help parents as they go through these adjustments?

Here is the issue for educators. A lot of times, up until the child is two or three, the parents may not know that there is a defined disability. (Sometimes, the parents may not know until the child is in kindergarten or even older.) The whole process of diagnosing what problems may be there is a very long, frustrating, and sometimes threatening process to go through. Often it's up to the teacher, particularly in the early years, to figure out what the strengths of the child are, what the weaknesses are, and if there are defined areas where the child needs help.

Part of the problem is the diagnostic side of this. A teacher is not a physician, and you don't want the teacher to be in the position of feeling that she's responsible for diagnosing the potential problems, whatever they may be. You don't want a teacher to look at every child as a diagnostic puzzle. In nursery school a lot of things can emerge, and the earlier it is diagnosed, the better. It's easier to get at that challenge when the child is five than when he is seven or eight.

The whole diagnostic process, then, is one that needs to be a kind of team effort. It should start, certainly, with the parents. However, if there is a strong element of denial, the teacher can play an important role in persuading the parents (if there is a problem) that the child needs to be tested or to receive physical therapy or whatever.

How can teachers most effectively communicate this kind of information?

It's real tough. It's always hard when you're a parent to listen to any kind of a problem connected with your child. The teacher is an authority figure for a parent and what she says carries a lot of weight. In listening to a teacher talk about a child, it's helpful to the parents if:

• It's done on a one-to-one sit down level in a non-threatening way.

• It takes place in person.

• The child is approached as an individual with many strengths. It's good for the parent to know what the teacher likes about the child. Things should be discussed in a constructive way.

• Words should be avoided that would be potentially threatening.

• Diplomacy is important. The teacher can be suggestive without coming down hard, without saying such and such is a problem. For example, teachers could say things like: "We see your child in just one of the many environments that he's in. These are just our observations. You, the parents, know him better than we do; we're just giving you some input. We do have the advantage of seeing 20 kids his age and stage every year, and you only have the opportunity of knowing him and a few other children his age. So we have that vantage point from which to share information with you." If the teacher approaches it from that standpoint, it's less threatening to the parent.

The other side of it is that the teacher has to level with the parent. If there is a problem, the parents need to know about it and do something to resolve it.

My child, David, has mild cerebral palsy. He wasn't walking at 18 or 19 months—but I was a late walker, so we didn't think one way or the other about it. I had a friend who said, "Look, David really should be checked out. He really looks like he might have a problem. Call. . . ." But there was a lot of denial there.

We took him to many doctors to figure out what the problem was. I had a terrible experience when I was sent to see an orthopedist who said to a resident, "Oh, this child obviously has mild cerebral palsy." I'd never heard the words cerebral palsy applied to my child! It was very difficult.

Then we thought, "We're not going to tell anybody because it will be a problem." But it was more that we were the ones who had the problem. We were the ones who were threatened, and it was that more than the fact that we were trying to protect David.

After David was diagnosed, a neighbor who was a priest suggested we call St. Columba's, because they have such a wonderful program which includes children with special needs.

How can teachers work with parents to provide the best experiences for children?

After the diagnosing, you get to the point of using an integrative approach. There are a lot of people who know the child in many different ways—teachers, parents, doctors, therapists. One of the tricks is to act as a catalyst to bring all these people together and to be the conduit of information that flows back and forth. All of these people have something to contribute and something to gain from listening to the others talking.

Even though St. Columba's has scheduled sessions with parents and teachers, I bring in the therapists. They talk about how David is doing and give each other suggestions: "Here's where David needs to be challenged" or "Don't push him in this area." And I send the doctor's reports to the school, so they are filled in and understand everything that's happening.

It's the parents' role to be the catalyst because parents are the only ones who know all the players. But if the parents don't pick up on it, the other way is for the teacher to try to play that role. The one big barrier the eacher has is if the parents are unwilling for whatever reason—they feel hreatened, or they don't want to spend the time, or whatever—to pull all his information together. It's very difficult for teachers to go beyond a ertain point. But they can encourage it to happen: "We know David is getting therapy. Could you send me any reports that the therapist has done, like some progress reports on how he's doing?"

The other approach teachers can take is to have parents get together and share some of these things. Maybe it's less threatening in a group than it is one to one. With any kind of problem, it's helpful to know that someone else has the same problem and to try to develop strategies together and learn from each other.

Last year, my husband, Jody, and I started a parenting group with parents from St. Columba's with children with identified special needs. We met once a month for six or seven sessions and covered a multitude of issues. Even though it was very beneficial for Jody and me personally and it worked out pretty well, we are not doing it this year. Once we went beyond a certain point, the issues became fragmented. The nature of the disability, the severity of the disability, how the child coped, how the parents coped all made the needs so diverse that we decided to take a different approach this year. This year there is a parenting group covering broader issues and within that context there may be a session that deals with parenting children with disabilities.

What things can an early childhood program do to bolster you as a parent?

At St. Columba's they have on their staff, as consultants, special education people who come in periodically to observe and to give feedback to the teachers. So there are other professionals teachers can turn to and people that teachers can draw into talking with parents. They're also available for parents. I found them to be very helpful, both from a technical standpoint and for psychological support.

St. Columba's looks at the child in a holistic way. They really hone in on the child's strengths and capabilities and potential. The child is encouraged to pursue avenues which will strengthen him as a person and allow him to grow. They transmit that to parents, and parents come away looking at their child a little bit differently.

We've grown a lot during the three years David has been at St. Columba's Nursery School. When he started the program I think we pampered him. I worked full time and we had a person full time taking care of him. She was wonderful and loving and, because of her great affection for David, she didn't push him quite as much as she could have. When we started

St. Columba's, it was like night and day. They expected him to get his coat on, to take his coat off, to unsnap his pants when he went to the bathroom, and that sort of thing. And they said to us, very gently but very clearly, "Look, David can be doing more things than he's doing. He can take his coat on and off. We'll show you the way." They insisted on our challenging him more; and they did it by saying, "We know that David can do such and such and you should begin to insist that he do some of these things at home." That was very helpful.

When David was there the first year, I didn't really have the time to get

Photograph by Subjects and Predicates

quite as involved with things going on at the school. They never put
pressure on me to do that. Now I was thinking maybe they should have
encouraged me to spend more time in the school. But that's really not
their role. I was being a good mother. The program has to accept the
realities within each family. One mother may have more time to spend
with her child than another. It's important for parents to know that
teachers are not standing in judgment of them.

What do you think the program is like for your son?

There are two children with special needs in each class of 18 children.
The structure is multifaceted—they don't stress just academics, just
motor, or just psychological. The main objective is to make the child feel
good about himself or herself and to bolster confidence and a sense of
curiosity about themselves, other people, and their environment. They do
it by being positive, by having an enthusiastic outlook. It's very
contagious.

David, during the first year, was very shy. He wasn't sure of himself.
Motorwise, he was very limited in what he would try to do. Over the
three years, he's become much more outgoing, much more confident. He
tries to do a lot more things, and they've encouraged him to try and not to
worry if he fails. The trick is to try and if you fail, that's okay—you just
get up and keep going. I think they've made him much more resilient in a
lot of ways, personally, with others, motorwise; he's motivated to
experiment.

They're very loving. It's one thing to challenge a child and try to
encourage a child to try different things, but then you need to be there to
have that net of support if the child needs to fall back or needs that
reassurance. So you need both of those things. If you have only one or
the other, it's not good. You need a balance.

The challenge for the teacher is to treat each child as an individual, to
seek out differences and to be equitable. But if you treat everyone the
same, you are not making use of each child's uniqueness. So you need to
seek out and recognize the differences and to help the child feel
comfortable with his own differences. The goal is to develop an
appreciation for each child as an individual and then to help parents
value their child as an individual.

Having a disabled child presents a lot of challenges. It really tests the
strengths of the parents and the child and forces all to come to terms with
being different and what that really means. The disability, which at first
seems so significant, somewhat embarrassing, and difficult to acknowledge, slowly diminishes in importance as the individuality of the

child emerges. David is witty, loving, bright, autonomous, and head-strong. I don't know to what extent his cerebral palsy has influenced his personality, but it is one of many facets of his life.

The disability will always be there. He once asked if he will always have cerebral palsy. I told him, "Yes, but it will improve through therapy and your own ability to deal with it." He cried about it, and I cried with him because it was a sad reality for us both. This was a year ago and I think that moment was a turning point. Openly acknowledging the disability has been helpful for all of us, and it must remain an open subject. However, everyone in the family feels that it is not the main focus or characteristic that defines David or that defines our role as his parents.

The issue of David's disability cannot be resolved at any one stage, because at each phase of development implications of the cerebral palsy will present themselves in different forms. However, my husband and I believe that it is our job to make him feel good about himself, to make him feel that he can accomplish almost anything he sets his mind to, and that we will be there if he needs us.

Meg Robinson is a free lance consultant specializing in marketing, strategic planning, and microcomputers. Her children are David, age 5, who has mild cerebral palsy, and Joshua, age 18 months; her third child is due in July.

Chapter Five
Living in a Changing World

"I don't think I'm different." Richard Koen in **The Wall Street Journal**, January 16, 1987.

The Impact of Current Changes in Social Structure on Early Childhood Education Programs

by Gail Raymond and Dean K. McIntosh

Mrs. Williams has decided to return to preschool teaching after an absence of 15 years. On her first day in the classroom, she arrives at 6:45 as she is anxious to be the first one there. Her initial shock is to find two three year olds sitting patiently on the front step of the school. Their parents, both working mothers, left them there at 6:30 so they could be to work on time.

Recovering from this shock (this never would have happened 15 years ago), she goes inside with the arriving staff. Much to her surprise, the next three children to arrive are all immigrant and refugee children who speak no English, nor do their parents. Another child is brought in by an elderly grandparent who has sole responsibility for the child during the day, as he is retired and the mother has moved home after a recent divorce.

Finally, things feel normal again, as several middle class children arrive who are more like the children she remembers. However, the next child to arrive is not dressed properly, smells, and has a cold. She looks for the mother, but learns that he has been transported and left at the doorstep by a social service agency.

As the morning progresses, she discovers that the children come from a mixture of low, middle, and upper middle income families. They are of various ethnic backgrounds, some speak no English, some have mothers who are in their teens, and many come from single family homes. She feels she is in a time warp; but, no, she has entered the present day and real world of early childhood education.

During recent years this country has experienced dramatic modifications in social structure. The size and composition of socio-economic classes have changed markedly, with concomitant changes in family structure. Whereas early childhood programs traditionally have been developed on the basis of a stereotyped middle class perspective on society and the family, this approach must now be reexamined in light of contemporary social changes.

Current Changes in Social Structure

Many educators continue to view children in terms of traditionally assumed socio-economic groupings. Even as late as the mid-1960's, there were three well-defined levels reported in the literature and used by most economists and sociologists—lower, middle, and upper classes, with differentiation usually based upon combinations of factors such as personal income, place of residence, profession, and educational background. During recent years, however, these classes have changed dramatically in size and structure due to rapid technological changes, civil rights and feminists movements, population shifts, expansion of mass communications, and job relocation, to name just a few of the causative factors. These changes have resulted in a shrinking of the middle class and an expansion of the lower class, with the poor becoming even poorer.

Even though these changes in social class structure have occurred, schools in general have failed to respond to these shifts and continue to function under the *middle class syndrome*—for the most part, teachers, the curriculum in the schools, and even the schools' philosophy reflect the emphasis found in the traditional middle class of the 1960's. Middle class has served as a hallmark and standard for the rest of society almost from the beginning of these United States.

To this day educators have long-standing preconceived ideas regarding the make-up of each of these three economic levels; these beliefs, in turn, have influenced the overall approach used in providing education to all children. The **low income family** is stereotypically viewed as one in which poverty is evident; there is often an unmarried mother, with a stable male model usually absent. There are many children at home, whose age range may be quite large. The house is usually substandard and most often is rented from an absentee landlord who cares little about keeping up the structure. Medical care and overall health of the children tends to be much below that of children in other socio-economic groups, as the parents must depend upon *free* medical care which involves numerous confusing forms to fill out and long waiting lines. There is little or no hope for the future as the poverty tends to be self-perpetuating. The poor are seen as lacking skills and educational opportunities which lead to economic opportunity. Their fight to survive on a day-to-day basis consumes all available energy.

The stereotype of the **middle class** is primarily of the two-parent family, with both parents living at home and the father being the major wage

Income Statistics

Rose (S. J. Rose, **The American Profile Poster,** New York:
Pantheon Books, 1986) has demonstrated that the middle class
has diminished markedly between 1978 and 1986, with 2.8
percent of that group entering the *high budget* group and 5.2
percent moving into the *low budget* and *poverty* groups. Families with children have constituted the bulk of those Americans
moving into the poorer socio-economic class.

Rose also pointed out that there has been a sharp income redistri-
bution from poor to rich among families with children between
1968 and 1983, with the lowest fifth of families with children
receiving 7.4 percent of cash family incomes in 1968 and 4.8
percent in 1983, and the highest fifth receiving 33.8 percent in
1968 and 38.1 percent in 1983.

The number of poor children jumped 30 percent between 1979 and
1984, while their participation in two key federal programs
dropped sharply during the same period. The rate of participation in Head Start and Aid to Families with Dependent Children
(AFDC) fell more than 20 percent during this five year period
and the number of poor children jumped from 9.9 million to 12.9
million ("Study Says Young Poor Count Up," **The State,** October
1986, p. 14.). Stated differently, 22 percent of all children now
reside in households with an income below the poverty line,
whereas during the 1970's the poverty rate for children
remained between 14 and 16 percent.

earner. If the mother works, it is for one express purpose—to help with
the expenses of a college education. Although there are several income
levels within the middle class, all the parents share the same dream of a
better life for their children. Economic opportunity, for this group, is
unalterably linked to a college education. It is presumed that a better
life with more money is the goal of most middle class parents.

The **upper class** stereotype is the fortunate few who are free from
economic worry. The lives of both of the parents are filled with many
civic and philanthropic activities, all of which take both time and
money. Upper class children are believed to be raised by full-time
housekeepers or regularly employed babysitters. They attend elite public
or private schools and are expected to carry on the family name and
tradition.

Since the beginning of free public education in the United States,
teachers have held these concepts of social structure and have geared

education primarily to the middle class. Educators have considered the middle class to be the primary supporter of schools, both emotionally and through taxes, and the middle class has been seen as the main beneficiary of public-provided educational opportunities. Curriculum traditionally has not been geared to the needs of the lower class, as the idea has been to educate this group to move into the middle class of society. The upper class was not considered to need the attention of the public schools as many of the children attended private schools. Those upper class children who attended public schools were in the *better* schools in the district where the curriculum and extracurricular experiences were rich and varied. In addition, their economic status was guaranteed, and they would benefit little from a formal education like the middle and lower class students.

These preconceived ideas of social class composition and class-related educational needs are not consistent with the realities of the mid-1980's. The boundaries between these groups have begun to change as the middle class has shrunk, the lower class has expanded, and the poor have become even more destitute. As rapid social mobility has occurred, the composition of each class has changed, and traditional stereotypes of classes do not fit.

Changes in socio-economic status can occur rapidly (see box on page 116). The following case examples demonstrate the rapidity of social mobility, potentially in either direction, though more often downward.

A middle income steel worker in a middle class community has worked for a local textile/steel mill since he graduated from high school. He is 35 years of age with four children, the youngest 2 and the oldest 16. One Friday he receives notification that his job will be abolished the following Friday. Overnight the family moves from middle income to lower income, and may soon appear on the welfare rolls for an extended period of time as they have little savings. This man has only specialized skills learned in the mill over the last 17 years, and he lacks the fundamental educational skills needed to participate successfully in a retraining program.

A different example is the 37 year old wife of a professional man. She and her husband live in an upper income golf club community. She is told by her husband that he is filing for divorce. They have three children, ages 6 months to 10 years. She holds a mater's degree in English literature, received 13 years ago. She has never been employed outside the home. The family, although in the upper income level, has limited savings and few investments other than the home, which has little equity in it. She is forced to move the children into a two bedroom apartment while seeking employment. She quickly realizes that her degree earned many years ago is useless in today's business world.

The child support provided by the father barely meets the essentials for the daily living standard acquired over the past 13 years. She has found herself, probably permanently, in the lower middle income group. The type of employment immediately available will be close to the minimum wage in a position that will allow little, if any, upward economic and social mobility in the near future.

A third example is the career oriented couple. The father is a business executive and the mother an account executive with a local advertising firm. The jobs of both demand extremely long hours of work each day. In addition, extended periods of business travel, entertaining of clients, and being visible at civic functions are all part of the job responsibilities. Their child attends an expensive child care program and spends many evenings and weekends with babysitters. Both parents are well aware of the need to be *good parents* and try, whenever possible, to spend time with their child. Both are big believers in *quality time* in which what limited time is available is well organized and intensive. Unfortunately, they fail to realize that *quantity time* is also important. This upwardly mobile, and rapidly growing, segment of today's society of career-oriented parents too often lacks both the time and energy to be interested in anything more than the child's overall academic development.

Such changes in socio-economic status, for better or worse, often take place very abruptly and dramatically, allowing the family little time to make any preparations for the changes. For a vast majority, any change of economic level is going to be negative and often irreversible, or at least long term in nature. While the move up the economic ladder is often slow, the move down can be very rapid and catastrophic in its impact upon the family structure.

The data and realities refute traditionally held assumptions about society that have influenced early childhood education programs today. It is inappropriate for a preschool teacher to subscribe to the traditional *middle class orientation* and structure her teaching of all children around this. There are several problems with this traditional approach. First, it was **never** valid to stereotype children from certain classes and assume that they had certain strengths or weaknesses based on their background and environment. While poorer children may lack opportunities that are available to other children, each child must be seen as an autonomous person and his/her abilities must be individually assessed. Second, with the shrinking of the middle class, more and more children are entering the lower socio-economic group; it would be irrelevant to teach all children using an approach geared to a fictional middle class group of children. With busing across neighborhoods and with the quick shifting of entire groups of children into lower income groups, few teachers have a purely middle class group of students. Third, with the fluid nature of today's society, even if a teacher has a group of predominantly middle class children at the beginning of the year, this could change by the end of the year. For example, an industry's closing could send entire school districts into poverty.

In addition to these social class shifts that have occurred in recent years, there are other contemporary trends in family structure that have implications for the preschool teachers. These changes also repudiate the use of a middle class perspective in developing early childhood

---

Current Trends

By the year 2000, one-third of all people in the United States will be non-White (C. G. Williams, "Population Trends Affect Education," **South Carolina School Board's Association Journal**, 1986, pp. 20-21).

Currently 20 percent of all children live in female headed households (U.S. Bureau of Census, **Marital Status and Living Arrangements—Current Population Report** [Series p. 20, No. 52], Washington, DC: Author, March 1981). Three-fifths (60 percent) of all children born in 1986 will spend at least part of their lives in a single parent family, with 90 percent of these being headed by females ("Deceptive Picture: Despite Signs to the Contrary, A Comeback by the Old Style Family Isn't Likely," **The Wall Street Journal**, September 1986, p. 22).

One-fifth (21.5 percent) of all children born in 1985 were unmarried mothers compared to 7.7 percent in 1965. The rate is rapidly increasing, especially with teenage pregnancies ("Deceptive Picture," 1986).

By the year 1990, the traditional family—consisting of a working father, a full-time housewife mother, and two or more children—will constitute only 6 percent of families (L. G. Baruth and M. Z. Burggraf, "The Counselor and Single Parent Families," **Elementary School Guidance and Counseling**, 19 (1), 1984, pp. 30-37.)

Poverty has rapidly become feminized with 57 percent of the Americans officially in poverty being female. There are now 3.6 million poor families with a female head of household, up 82 percent from 1960 (Rose, 1986).

programs. The structure of the American family is changing, and it is not appropriate for teachers to view their students in terms of traditional stereotypical ideas of the family. While some of these changes in family structure may be in opposition to the presently held values of educators, they should be aware of these developments and take them into consideration when planning curriculums. Many of these trends have been known for the past ten years, yet educators have done little to address their impact in planning early childhood programs.

These changes in social class structure and the current trends in family composition suggest that preschool teachers may need to modify some of their theoretical perspectives and, consequently, change some of their approaches to teaching. The use of a middle class perspective in designing and implementing preschool programs is not valid and teachers must develop their programs in light of current changes in social class and family structure.

Implications for Early Childhood Programs

The changes in social class and family composition described above should influence the design of curriculum for early childhood programs as well as the approaches used in assessing the strengths, weaknesses, and needs of each individual child.

Curriculum design. If by the year 2000 one-third of all United States residents will be non-White, it is very important for early childhood programs to expose children to various ethnic groups through real-life experiences and program content and materials. In California, for example, all children need great amounts of exposure to Chicanos and their way of life. Early and positive exposure to many ethnic groups is essential to help children become aware of the ethnic groups around them and their relationship to other ethnic groups.

In addition to the increase of non-White citizens, there continues to be an influx of immigrant and refugee children from all parts of the world, especially Southeast Asia and South and Central America. The parents know the importance of education and of becoming a part of the system, so they quickly place their children in available preschool programs. Many of these children speak no English when they enter a program, and their parents speak little more than rudimentary English. Teachers face the necessity of gaining skills in teaching English to non-English speaking children. They must also work with these parents regarding the type of education offered to young children, for it may be very different from the expectations they had for their children in their native countries.

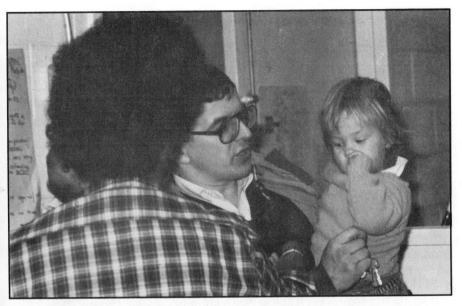

Photograph by Subjects and Predicates

The teacher can seek experts within the community who have in-depth knowledge about the various cultures and ethnic groups that are represented within the classroom, such as church members who are involved in sponsoring refugees from Southeast Asia. Experts within social service agencies or local colleges and universities, and the parents themselves, are also resources.

With approximately 60 percent of all children facing the prospect of living in single parent homes—most often with their mothers—the curriculum should be designed to assist these children in validating their family situation. Far too often young children only hear about, and see representations of, the traditional family situation which makes it extremely difficult for them to understand how their own family situation correlates with what they are hearing and seeing.

By the same token, if males are becoming less present and involved within certain family structures, it is important that children of both sexes be provided with positive male images and role models at this early age. Greater impact of male guests and helpers and the presence of men as teachers in child care programs are all needed. And there is the need to select materials which reinforce images of men, as well as women, in a broad spectrum of roles.

Stepparents and grandparents are playing increasingly significant caretaking roles in the lives of many young children. It may be that the only feasible economic solution for a separated and/or divorced parent is to return home to parents. Grandparents may have to assume the major responsibility for the raising of the grandchildren while the parent works. Regardless of the situation, positive images of stepparents and grandparents should be present in materials and curriculum.

Increasing numbers of children of teenage mothers will be present in preschool programs, and it becomes necessary to involve the teenage mothers in the educational process in a different way. Many of these mothers will reside in homes in which there are no adult males and where the mother of the teenager may also have very young children. It may well be that neither of the two ever gained the skills of motherhood and thus there is no passing down of these skills. The preschool teacher can assume a significant role in assisting these young mothers in developing good parenting skills.

Informal assessment. Socio-economic factors have an impact on all children even before they come to school; however, most children still arrive ready and excited to learn. They bring their own experiences from the home and community, which may be rich and varied or extremely limited. Nevertheless, each child brings something. It is important that teachers determine what skills and knowledge the child has already acquired, identify what each child needs to learn, and plan how best to meet those needs.

Assessing each child's developmental skills can assist the teacher in deciding what and how to teach and when to teach it. In this approach, the teacher is assessing a child's skill development for instructional planning. It does not tell why the child has certain skills already and does not have others, nor does it tell what socio-economic level or background experiences are brought to the school. It does tell the teacher where the child is now and helps her decide how to best meet the learning needs of each child.

Parent communication. For many parents, especially those who are recent immigrants or refugees, the school is an alien place. In many of the third world countries, education has been reserved for the *elite* and few children of middle and almost none from lower income families are given the opportunity to attend school. Because members of the family may have a long history of non participation in the school systems, they may have little or no understanding of their roles and responsibilities. Even for native parents, there may often be a great deal of hesitation to become involved in their children's education for a variety of reasons—fear of being perceived as pushy and demanding, lack of time and energy, feelings of guilt and uncertainty.

For many parents, learning how to work successfully with early childhood teachers will profoundly affect the education of all their children throughout their schooling. Also, by establishing an open channel of communication with parents, teachers can share important information at an early stage and avoid some of the problems that may arise later.

It falls to the teacher to initiate this communication, and it continues to be a teacher's responsibility until parents feel secure enough to initiate contacts on their own. In some situations the parents may never feel secure enough to take the first step, and the only alternative is for the teacher to continue to take the lead.

Harsh realities. After all the theories have been expounded and the rhetoric presented, teachers of young children must face the realities of Monday morning. It is extremely helpful for every teacher to have an updated resource guide to the community, which may be available through a local college or agency or assembled and updated by the teachers themselves. Knowledge of community support services, such as food and clothing banks, is helpful in meeting the needs of children who may arrive at school with less than adequate family support at home.

Conclusion

It is important for the early childhood teacher to be aware of and constantly reexamine the assumptions on which her program is based. Outdated or invalid beliefs will result in programs that are not relevant to the needs of the children. Current changes in socio-economic structures in the United States challenge many previously held assumptions. Teachers must abandon a middle class orientation towards education, shed stereotyped notions about family structure, and cease making assumptions about a child's learning needs based on the child's background. The design of an early childhood curriculum and the determination of each child's strengths and weaknesses must be based upon a realistic view of contemporary society and an individual assessment of each child.

Gail Raymond is a professor in the Department of Educational Psychology at the University of South Carolina, Columbia, South Carolina. Dean K. McIntosh is an associate professor in the Department of Educational Psychology at the University of South Carolina.

Children Are Caught—
Between Home and School,
Culture and School

by Betsy West

Though diversity of experience and culture is educative, it may also contribute to increased difficulties for a classroom teacher. When the values and habits of the parents differ significantly from those of the school and teacher, there is unspoken conflict between the two and the child is caught in that conflict. First, let it be noted that teachers should anticipate such conflicts because most teachers have internalized middle class mores and customs (whether or not they were actually reared in middle class homes); yet most of the children in their care are likely not from middle class homes. (See statistics and comments about downward mobility in Raymond article, page 114.)

Second, the conflict may seem keener in schools which serve young children because they have not yet learned to *play the system* as well as older children, to pretend conformance to expectations different from those they are used to. Also, it may be more difficult to explain value or cultural conflicts to younger children than it is to older ones. (If the truth be told, however, few teachers of older children try to explain cultural conflicts; they just demand that the student play by their rules when at school.)

Certainly, many differences in children are individual differences, but some differences arise because their sub-cultures, ethnicity, or family lifestyles are unlike those of the school and teacher. Understanding those background factors may help teachers preclude problems generated by the differences or at least find more satisfactory means of coping with those problems.

Individual vs. Group

In the United States we glorify individualism, and (at least verbally) we also glorify cooperation, without admitting that sometimes those two values are contradictory. Preschool children may come from homes where both values are stressed, but frequently certain ethnic groups stress cooperation and even communal ownership more than middle class Anglos do. In child care programs teachers expect both individualism and cooperation, but it is often unclear to the child when we expect which.

At home and at school we give children mixed signals about sharing. "Share your toys with your friends," but when a visiting child breaks an expensive toy, it's "I told you you'd have to take care of your toys. . . . Yes, I told you to share, but why did you let him play with *that* toy?" At school we say, "Share the playground equipment," "Take your turn in line" (and we have lots of lines in schools), "You can both play in the house corner," etc. Still, many of our activities are designed for individual work or play. Even the colorful charts in our classrooms seem to teach competition rather than cooperation. It's how many smiling faces are beside one name as compared to someone else's. Children from certain cultural groups have been taught that the group is always more important than the individual and that it is wrong to draw attention to one's self even by an outstanding achievement.

Mine is often one of the first words of middle class children, but some children never think in terms of *my* crayons, *my* room. They have been taught that ownership is by the group rather than the individual. At school, then, using or even taking crayons or a pencil from another is not considered stealing. Children from a relatively communal subculture or from extreme poverty, who may share a single coat or pair of shoes with siblings, simply cannot perceive taking another's lunch in the same way that a middle class child would perceive it. Yet, we as teachers sometimes behave as though we believe children are born understanding the concept of private ownership. When we so carefully give each child his own space or particular supply of materials, are we teaching private ownership or are we teaching selfishness? Indeed, where do we want to draw the line between the two?

Family Patterns

One of the differences between a child's perception and that of the teacher may be the concept of family. Recently, during a lull in a show-and-tell group, Karen said something to Kia which prompted her friend to respond, "Ask your daddy." Karen replied, "I ain't got a daddy," but almost immediately grinned and said, "Oh, that's right. I'm going to get a new daddy next week." Kia announced, "Teacher, teacher! Karen's mommy is getting married next week." Karen corrected her: "No, she's not. I just get a new daddy every two or three months."

The teacher, conservative in her lifestyle and beliefs, and with only a few years of teaching experience, was flustered by the comment and feared discussion of any controversial issues. She quickly cancelled the rest of the show-and-tell time and immediately put the children to work on quiet readiness workbooks. That was much safer.

The teacher's body language and change of attitude must have implied to the child that something was wrong with what happened at her house. Somewhere, sometime, concerned teachers have to let children know that there are different groupings of people called family, that love and care are the important elements in a family, that there are families without fathers, families without mothers, families of two adults of the same gender, and so on. There are various ways to do this in the curriculum and its activities, but the crucial part is for the teacher to be respectful of the differences presented and of the different environments from which children come.

The rate of serial monogamy continues to increase, and there are many reasons to be concerned about that phenomena—reasons which do indeed affect children. But the child is not in a position to change those trends. We know that the self-concept of young children is largely developed by significant others in their lives. What we as teachers sometimes fail to realize is that we may damage the child's self-concept when we are critical, overtly or covertly, of those who are the significant persons in that child's life.

Sex Roles

Even though family patterns and arrangements are changing (more single parent families, more working parents, etc.), many American families continue to teach traditional sex roles. Confusion may arise, therefore, when the child enters a child care program where boys are encouraged to cook and dress up and girls are encouraged to play with blocks, trucks, and road equipment. Again, how these differences are handled is more important than the fact that there are differences.

To the boy who says, "My daddy don't want me to play with dolls 'cause that's sissy," we can easily respond: "I bet your father loved you when you were a baby just as he loves you now. Pretending the doll is your baby is really pretending you are a grown man who can be a daddy." And we can casually tell the father what we've said without demanding an attitudinal change on his part.

In an age when more emphasis is rightly put on androgyny, teachers need to remember that gender identification is still a necessary part of the child's maturing process. It is possible that some teachers stress broader, non-traditional roles for boys more than they do for girls. In observing a preschool for an entire semester, I often saw the teacher and ides encourage boys to play in the house corner, to dress up, to cook, but I didn't see equal encouragement for the girls to become involved in non-traditional roles. When the girls themselves initiated play with *boys'* *toys*, the teachers protected their rights to take turns, but I did not see the active encouragement of girls to play telephone repair person, ambulance driver, or fire fighter. Indeed the girls were sometimes given considerable approval (albeit with bemusement) when they dressed up and assumed grown-up (coquettish) manners of walking, etc. Again, this is an area in which preschool teachers need to look at themselves very carefully. Do we want males to change their roles more than we want females to change theirs? Or is it only that female educators want this more?

Ethnicity

Some of the differences children reflect result from their ethnic or cultural experience. We must be careful not to assume that children of similar racial/ethnic backgrounds are compatible. There are social class differences and personality differences within each ethnic and racial group. We must remember that other countries also have stratification. A child may refer to another from his native land as *just a* *fisherman* in the same manner that Americans refer to a stereotypical *hillbilly*. We may assume similarities that may not be there. We assume the Asian children should be compatible and helpful to each other or that the Blacks should get along with each other. Why? Goodness knows many Whites don't get along with each other. With immigrant children it may be more helpful to ask a child who is a native speaker of English to be the *partner*.

School Activities

Sometimes it is the school activities themselves which are the subject of differences with parents. Most early childhood educators at least give lip service to Dewey's concept that one of the purposes of education is to broaden the child's experience, his/her horizons. In trying to achieve that goal, however, we may find ourselves in conflict with the more narrow perceptions of the home environment and in conflict with parents who actually do not want the experiences of their children to include anything which doesn't reinforce the habits and values of home.

All early childhood educators know about the values of water play, finger painting, and other messy activities. The well known Sexsmith Demonstration Preschool in Vancouver, British Columbia, used such activities in meaningful and educative ways. But some of their students came from traditional Chinese backgrounds. Because schooling was extremely important, the little girls were dressed in their

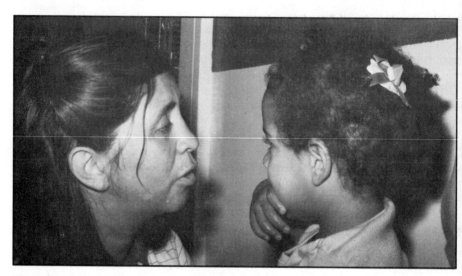

Photograph by Subjects and Predicates

finest clothes to come to school, not the jeans and t-shirts of their Canadian peers. By the end of the day their dresses were frequently splattered with paint.

The primary child care of one Chinese girl lay with a grandmother who was perhaps 60 when she had immigrated. This grandmother certainly didn't expect such messiness at school, and she was further confused about why parents were invited to the school so frequently. From her point of view, teachers were the experts and shouldn't have parents telling them what to do. Nonetheless, she tried to meet the educators' expectations and eventually yielded to their urgings to express her feelings. Though her English was minimal, she made her point in no uncertain tone: "School too messy. Water and paint make too much ironing pretty dresses. School learning better from books."

That grandmother did not share the educators' ideas of learning and she certainly didn't want her grandchild wearing jeans to school, though that seemed to the teachers to be the easiest solution. Note that th first solution they thought of meant that someone else should do the changing or compromising. It is to their credit that they caught themselves and offered to send notes home to inform the parents when there would be exceptionally messy activities—and I expect they were more careful to see that children were attired in their aprons.

Language

The language which children hear outside of school often differs from what they hear at school or what the teacher considers appropriate.

Early childhood teachers have long noted the variety of euphemisms which children from different backgrounds use for genitalia and excretion. Sometimes they accept the child's usage, sometimes they add their own euphemisms, sometimes they gradually substitute more scientific labels. In spite of this familiarity with different usage, however, teachers sometimes show their surprise or disdain when the words come up at times other than bathroom breaks.

In a lesson about animals and the sounds they make, the teacher mentioned felines. She referred to a domestic cat as "kitty-cat" and later said "pussy." At that point, however, a student told her, "Hell, Miz Murdock, pussies don't make noise; they're for other things." The fact that few students laughed did not alleviate Ms. Murdock's shock.

If teachers consider levels of usage a necessary concept for children to learn if they are to function in broader segments of society than the one in which they are reared, they do have to explain that some people use different terms and that some terms are considered inappropriate in certain settings. Still this *correction* must be done without putting down the child who uses the terms as he has heard and learned them.

Orderliness

The degree of organization and order varies greatly among families— and also among teachers. Even so, most child care programs and their teachers necessarily have considerable organization of time, space, materials, and activities. If children come from homes where *a place for everything and everything in its place* is the practice, the children respond easily to similar demands in school. But if the child is from a home where there are no toys, it may seem like punishment to have to put away all the toys, including his/her favorite, even for story hour. Children who live in homes in which belongings are casually piled in disarray may not be able to understand the teacher's *obsession* with order.

The structure of time may be another part of this problem. Middle class children will have already had considerable experience with their parents keeping schedules and making appointments. They will have been a part of planning for the future and delayed gratification: "Take your nap and we'll go to the park." "Eat your vegetables and you can have dessert." They are likely to be more cooperative as we try to get the classroom decorated before parents' night or some other deadline.

To children who have come from families preoccupied with surviving from day to day, it may seem foolhardy to interrupt current play for some future good (like a party connected with parents' night) that they

and their parent(s) may be unable to attend. Such lack of cooperation
can be quite disruptive to the goals of the group and annoying to the
teacher. In reality, such children simply have not had the socialization
for school which some of their middle class peers have had.

Locale

Children in any kind of preschool or child care live in a more confined
space than do rural children. There are fences around their yards, and
implicit in every fence or physical barrier is a notion that someone or
something must be kept in or out. Early childhood educators conscien-
tiously take children on walks to explore the neighborhood or the park.
But isn't that a euphemism? We may be allowing them to observe—a
worthwhile and educative experience. We point out various plants,
colors, building, but explore? Hardly. We want them to hold the hands
of their partners; we don't want them to go in someone's yard (we have
to teach the concept of private property); we want to cover the planned
route in the allowed time.

A child who had spent his entire five years in a megalopolis recently
visited a grandmother whose home is on a small creek in a city. She
took him to explore the shoreline, through the adjoining yard of
neighbors (whom, in fact, she didn't know). But it was the child who
kept looking and saying, "This isn't your yard. Will they get us for
being here?" There were attitudes to overcome before his curiosity
turned to the holes and rocks, plants, color, birds, and mud of the shore.

As a high-rise resident, I watched a father play ball with his son every
night—in a space about three feet square which bordered a busy street. It
was pleasing to watch their interaction, but I kept thinking how that
experience was developing that child's notion of space. He would
probably be like an eight year old I know who begs to go to the shopping
mall after the stores close: "The mall is a place to run!" There is no
place in urban or suburban America for children to run freely.
Imagine such a child turned loose in a pasture or field. Even with the
best of visuals and children's stories, how can we explain suburban or
rural life to a child who has only lived in the inner city of Hong Kong,
San Francisco, or Miami?

Not only does locale influence a child's understanding of what space
means, it may also affect his awareness of noise and silence. One
school in Vancouver took a class on a field trip to a mountain so they
could see snow. They were impressed, but more striking was the open
space without buildings and the *quiet*. No background noise of traffic or
sounds of passersby. The quietness was as new to them as the snow.

Noise Level

Children who live in crowded circumstances may have a greater
tolerance for background noise than others. But most early childhood
teachers want absolute quiet while they give instructions or read a story.
We want to teach children that it is rude to speak when someone else is
speaking. On the other hand, the children in our classes today have
grown up in homes where everyone talks while the television is on,
particularly during commercials. Even the polite child may not
consider his behavior rude if he isn't drowning out the teacher.
Sometimes we're told, "Go ahead with the story, teacher. I'm just
talking to Juan." Television keeps on going, why can't teachers?

Tactility and Aggression

Early childhood teachers are often surprised at the degree of
physicalness of their children. Some teachers complain that certain
children *get right up* in their faces. Also, the degree of touching
considered common or acceptable varies greatly across ethnic and
social class lines. Children from large families may be more used to
considerable touching, but may resent touching by non-family. A
teacher who considers a pat on the head or shoulder as a sign of affection
may have it shrugged off quite vehemently or even squeamishly.
Among some children this preference for non-touching may come from
a strong sense of privacy which has been in their upbringing and, in
recent years, may have been intensified by parental reaction to media
reports of sexual abuse of children.

Sometimes of greater concern is tactility that is aggressive. Holding,
hitting, kicking, and biting may not just occur among peers, but may
also be directed at the teachers. This violates the middle class image of
respect due authority figures. And the openness and vehemence are
contrary to the middle class ideal of tone modulation and reserve.

Though we encourage noise and movement on the playground, we
expect children to shift to a much quieter and less active mode when they
are inside. This pattern of behavior may be a result of personality, but it
may also be a result of the child's observations and experience. We
should not be surprised that children who may see adults yell and hit at
each other also behave in this manner. If discussion is not the model
children have witnessed, how can we expect them to know how to talk out
their problems?

Further, some have been taught to *stand up and fight*: "Only sissies
don't fight back." "Stand up for your rights." "Punch his lights out if
he calls you that again." And those children are in groups with

children who have been told, "It takes two to make a fight" or "Don't hit back; the teacher can settle it." The conflicts arising from these two extremes are further confused by the contradictory messages (verbal and nonverbal, manifest and latent) which we as teachers give through our responses: punishing or shaming (either the aggressor or the victim) or helping each child see the consequence of his or her actions.

The degree of aggression to be tolerated is certainly an area which demands that teachers analyze their own educational philosophies. Do we want to let children see school rules are different from those at home, but just as authoritarian? Do we really want to show reasons for the rules—who made them, why, what would be the consequences of each? To what extent do we want to teach independence and self-reliance? Do we actually want to teach children to be concerned for the welfare of their peers or *to mind their own business*?

Sometimes we teachers criticize strict, authoritarian parents, but refuse to see that we are equally dogmatic about the rules of the classroom and school. If we would face the broader ethical questions in these dilemmas, instead of substituting one unquestionable authority for another, children would likely have more opportunity to advance through Kohlberg's levels of moral judgment. The tragedy is that the *good* students learn to meet expectations and play their roles in different situations—they learn to conform, not to reason. They learn how to accept discipline, not to self-discipline. Again the educational setting contributes to the mixed message of society rather than helping children understand the conflicts in human relations.

Peer Acceptance

If a child's background is similar to that of the teacher, the teacher may not even realize that understanding the culture is automatically part of the planning and teaching process. When our background is different from those of our students in any of the ways mentioned, it is necessary for us to be consciously aware of those backgrounds so that our planning and teaching processes are equally effective for all. Sometimes the differences are as basic as cleanliness, but have far broader implications.

"What of the unnurtured child? He is the child who comes to school dirty, with unbrushed teeth, smelly ears, filthy hair, and often unfed. The children single him out immediately, and at a very early age he becomes an observer rather than a participant in life. Social services is usually uninterested and unable to help this kind of child and is reluctant to become involved unless there is extreme neglect or abuse. I have found working with these parents has some positive effect, which usually lasts about one week, until the lifestyle patterns fall back in place. How does a child from this kind of home ever grow in self-esteem? Aside from patching (grooming at school, etc.), how can a professional be of help? I have watched these children remain outcasts— always on the edge of things, wishing, throughout their school years, and have found my own ability to help inadequate." (Diane Burger, kindergarten teacher at The Mountain School, Sun Valley, Idaho)

It's easy to feel that anyone can keep his/her children clean, but we must stop to think how much soap and laundromats cost. And we forget water is often shut off because of unpaid utilities. Realistically, teachers must admit that, short of adopting the individual child, they cannot solve all the social problems that affect children. But within the confines of the time and space we share with that child, we can arrange circumstances which provide opportunity for his/her participation and success. The hair may be stringy and the clothes dirty, but we can compliment the smile. We can do something about the self-concept, at least at school. And, gradually, the child can assume some responsibility for his/her own cleanliness.

The more difficult task is encouraging the other children to include them. We can demonstrate that we aren't afraid of getting close to the child: "I want to sit beside Emily today." We can choose that child as leader when they play follow the leader. We all know children can be unkind and alarmingly candid in expressing their distaste, but a part of our job as teachers is to teach them to respect others, beginning in our classrooms. We *can* guide the reactions of the other children.

Conclusion

Some differences between schools and home are unavoidable. It is not so much the differences themselves which are troublesome, but rather how the school personnel handle those differences. We can be understanding without agreeing. If we as teachers establish rapport with the children and their parents, if we earn the respect of the parents, if it is clear to children and parents that we care about them, if we take the time to explain our reasons for activities, if we give parents an opportunity to explain their points of view—if we do all those things, not just one or two, in most cases the parents will accept the policies and practices of the school.

At the height of the civil rights demonstrations, a parent said to me, "You and me ain't never going to agree about niggers, Mrs. West. But I do know that you love my boy, so you won't teach him nothing that will hurt him." Having already established positive relations with the child and his parents, I could then explain that their son was growing up in a world that would be different from the world they had known, that the school was trying to prepare him to function in that world.

In the most extreme cases, it may become necessary to say that parents have the right to teach their values to their children, but the school has the obligation to prepare children to function in a broader society. That may give the parents the responsibility for improving their teaching so that the child is presented two strong influences which educate the child. The teacher might point out she never tells the child that the parents are wrong, and it would be easier for the child if the parents didn't openly say the teacher is wrong.

For a few parents such a disagreement eventually may mean withdrawing their child from the school. Neither the school nor the individual teacher should abrogate their responsibility to the larger society nor to the task of preparing the child to function in the larger society. If we make the extra effort, in most cases we can find the communication skills to persuade or at the very least differ without being arrogant or disagreeable. Perhaps, sadly, we teachers are most dogmatic when we have weak points or secretly feel the parents aren't worth our time. I doubt that teachers can really love children if they hold the parents in contempt. If children are products of their experiences, so too are parents. And they likewise deserve respect and understanding.

Betsy West teaches social foundations of education and multicultural education at The Wichita State University, Wichita, Kansas. She recently spent a sabbatical in Vancouver observing the Sexsmith ESL Demonstration Preschool, Child Study Centre, University of British Columbia.

Chapter Six
Considering Our Resources

Has "the writer gone beyond and behind stereotypes, myths, and ideas . . . to develop characters whose ethnic, social, cultural, and personal experiences mesh in all the complex ways they do in real life . . ."? Judith Thompson and Floria Woodard in the **Wilson Library Bulletin**, December 1969.

What Are We Really Saying to Children? Criteria for the Selection of Books and Materials

by Bonnie Neugebauer

Children receive messages from myriad sources within the context of the early childhood environment. We must be conscious of the messages which come through our words and actions and silences, and we must evaluate the messages inherent in the materials we provide. Only when we are deliberately selecting and evaluating can we hope that the messages children receive while in our care are consistent with the philosophy and goals of our programs. (For a quick, easy way to evaluate your entire library/classroom, ask parents and other staff each to take a few books/materials and an equal number of photocopies of this checklist to review on their own.)

Look for the Messages in Children's Books

Evaluate the Characters

Yes No

- ☐ ☐ Do the characters in the story have personalities like real people?
- ☐ ☐ Do they seem authentic in the way they act and react?
- ☐ ☐ Do they speak in a style and language that fits their situation?
- ☐ ☐ Are they real people with strengths and weaknesses rather than stereotypes?
- ☐ ☐ Are characters allowed to learn and grow?
- ☐ ☐ Is their lifestyle represented fairly and respectfully?

Evaluate the Situation

- ☐ ☐ Do the characters have power over their own lives?
- ☐ ☐ Do they resolve their own problems and reap their own rewards?
- ☐ ☐ Are human qualities emphasized?

Evaluate the Illustrations

☐ ☐ Do the illustrations depict ethnic, age, cultural, economic, ability, and sexual differences respectfully? (Illustrations can be humorous, but they must fit the context of the story line and be consistent in portrayal.)

☐ ☐ Do the illustrations and the text work well together to communicate the story?

☐ ☐ Is the style of illustration appropriate to the story?

Evaluate the Messages

☐ ☐ Do the messages conveyed, both directly and indirectly, respectfully and accurately portray the human condition?

☐ ☐ Are there hidden messages which are demeaning in any way or which reinforce stereotypes?

Evaluate the Author/Illustrator's Credibility

☐ ☐ Does the author/illustrator's background and training prepare her or him to present this story? (Do not disregard, but do consider carefully, stories about women written by men, stories about people with handicaps written by people without handicaps, stories about one ethnic group written by another.)

Consider Your Selections as a Whole

It is not possible for any one book to portray all that we want to say to children, so it is important to look at your whole library:

☐ ☐ Are there stories about the contemporary life of a given ethnic group as well as tales and legends?

☐ ☐ Do the cultures represented in your library at least cover (and optimally extend well beyond) those cultures represented by the families in your program?

☐ ☐ Are there books in which the disability or racial or economic difference is just part of the context for a story about people's lives, as well as books which focus on that particular difference?

Look for the Messages in Materials and Equipment

☐ ☐ Does this toy stereotype people by sex, race, age, family situation, physical or intellectual skills?

☐ ☐ Does the selection of materials as a whole represent the
        diversity of humankind?
☐ ☐ How long will this toy hold a child's interest?
☐ ☐ Can it be adapted or used in different ways to change with
        different interests and ages of children?
☐ ☐ Can it be combined with other play materials to extend its
        possibilities?
☐ ☐ Is it safe, sturdy, appealing?
☐ ☐ Does the packaging of the toy reflect diversity? (If not, throw it
        away or use it for discussion, and write to the manufacturer.)
☐ ☐ Is the way in which children play with these materials
        consistent with your program's philosophy and goals?

Portions of these criteria were adapted from **Beginning Equal: A
Manual About Nonsexist Childrearing for Infants and Toddlers** *(New
York: Women's Action Alliance, Inc. and Pre-School Association, Inc.,
1983) and " 10 Quick Ways to Analyze Books for Racism and Sexism,"*
Council on Interracial Books for Children *(Volume 5, Number 3, 1974)*

Reflecting Diversity—
Books to Read with Young
Children

by Bonnie Neugebauer

Books and catalogs spill off the shelves, over my desk, and onto the floor. The topic we've chosen for this volume is so broad, there are so many pieces, so many ways that we can look at ourselves and others. Where do I begin to sort out the good from the bad, the enriching from the limiting? And even as I began the search for every book that includes through story or illustration ways in which we differ from each other, the gems that I am now searching for are those books which present people as people, including differences as a natural part of life, books which celebrate our humanity.

The ideal of this process would include an even distribution which in itself would reflect the spectrum, but as I worked and read, I realized that to even the distribution, I would have to make too many compromises. The following list is lopsided, with some holes and gaps; but the books it contains meet our criteria and represent what books for young children should be.

1. First of all, they are good stories. They are interesting both to read and to listen to.

2. The illustrations work with the text and in many, many instances are wonderfully delightful or breathtaking.

3. They meet the criteria for book selection set forth on page 136.

Illustrators, authors, and publishing companies have a long way to go to meet the needs of our children for wonderful stories which include children of all ethnic groups, all religious groups, all economic situations, all ability levels playing, living, working, problem-solving together, discovering their world and their individual and shared humanity.

So in your reading, if you discover a great story about a Jewish child in the midst of a sibling rivalry, a Hmong child using his art to sort out his life, an illustrator who includes handicapped people in her illustrations, remember that name! You have discovered a person who is trying to make a difference; spread the word!

Books Rich in Diversity

Ancona, George. **Helping Out.** New York: Clarion Books, 1985 ($12.95, hardback).

People of different ages can share a task and grow closer in the process. Photographs highlight diversity.

Andrews, Jan. **Very Last First Time** (illustrated by Ian Wallace). New York: Atheneum, 1985 ($11.95, hardback).

Eva is filled with the excitement of her first adventure collecting mussels beneath the thick sea ice.

Bang, Molly. **The Grey Lady and the Strawberry Snatcher.** New York: Four Winds Press, 1980 ($12.95, hardback).

A magical wordless fantasy which follows the Grey Lady's clever and surprising methods of eluding the Strawberry Snatcher who is always close.

Bang, Molly. **The Paper Crane.** New York: Greenwillow Books, 1985.

A hungry stranger brings new life to a fading restaurant in this story of generosity rewarded, based on an ancient folktale.

Baylor, Byrd. **Before You Came This Way** (illustrated by Tom Bahti). New York. E. P. Dutton & Co., 1969.

Prehistoric Indian rock drawings tell us of men who once lived on earth.

Baylor, Byrd. **Everybody Needs a Rock.** New York: Atheneum, 1974.

Baylor, Byrd. **The Way to Start a Day** (illustrated by Peter Parnall). New York: Aladdin Books, 1977 ($3.95, paperback).

Bourke, Linda. **Handmade ABC.** Reading, MA: Addison-Wesley Publishing Company, 1981 ($3.95, paperback).

Clear illustrations show how to hand sign each letter of the alphabet.

Children's Television Workshop (with Linda Bove). **Sign Language Fun** (illustrated by Tom Cooke). New York: Random House, 1980.

Photographs illustrate how to sign many words familiar and important to young children.

Clifton, Lucille. **The Boy Who Didn't Believe in Spring** (illustrated by Brinton Turkle). New York: E. P. Dutton, 1973.

Finding signs of spring in the city can be a difficult task, but doubters King Shabazz and Tony Polito set out to try.

Cooney, Barbara. **Miss Rumphius**. New York: Viking Penguin, 1985 ($4.95, paperback).

An independent young girl listens to her grandfather's advice and her own dreams. She travels the world, in old age lives by the sea, and eventually finds her own special way to make the world more beautiful.

Cooney, Nancy Evans. **The Wobbly Tooth** (illustrated by Marylin Hafner). New York: G. P. Putnam's Sons, 1978 ($2.95, paperback).

A loose tooth continues to annoy Elizabeth Ann throughout her spirited day.

Cummings, Pat. **Jimmy Lee Did It**. New York: Lothrop, Lee & Shepard Books, 1985 ($11.75, hardback).

Brother Artie blames Jimmy Lee for all kinds of disasters and evil deeds; but when Angel tries to catch him, he's always a step ahead of her.

de Paola, Tomie. **Watch Out for the Chicken Feet in Your Soup.** Englewood Cliffs, NJ: Prentice-Hall,1974 ($4.95, paperback).

Joey is jealous when his grandma gives his friend too much attention.

Dragonwagon, Crescent. **Half a Moon and One Whole Star** (illustrated by Jerry Pinkney). New York: Macmillan Publishing Company, 1986 ($12.95, hardback).

A wonderful soothing rhythm pulses through the night as Susan falls asleep and the creatures and people of the night awake.

Father Gander (Dr. Douglas W. Larche). **Father Gander Nursery Rhymes** (illustrated by Carolyn). Advocacy Press, PO Box 236, Santa Barbara, CA 93102 ($12.95, hardback), 1985.

People seem to react strongly one way or the other to this rewrite of Mother Goose rhymes. Verses added to the original rhymes give equal time to both sexes. Illustrations superbly reflect diversity and include handicapped children—for this alone it deserves kudos.

Gauch, Patricia Lee. **Christina Katerina & The Box** (illustrated by Doris Burn). New York: Coward, McCann & Geoghegan, 1971.

Christina has plenty of imagination as she and her friend Fats explore the play potential of a large cardboard carton.

Greene, Jacqueline Dembar. **Nathan's Hanukkah Bargain** (illustrated by Steffi Karen Rubin). Kar-Ben Copies, Inc., 6800 Tildenwood Lane, Rockville, MD 20852, 1986 ($4.95, paperback; $10.95 hardback).

Nathan invites his grandfather to help him shop for a menorah, but it takes some effort and a little bargaining to find just the right one.

Greenfield, Eloise. **Daydreamers** (illustrated by Tom Feelings). New York: Dial Books for Young Readers, 1985 ($3.95, paperback).

Intriguing sketches of black children fill out the poem's images of children who pause for reflection.

Greenfield, Eloise. **Darlene** (illustrated by George Ford). New York: Methuen, 1980 ($7.95, hardback).

Greenfield, Eloise. **First Pink Light** (illustrated by Moneta Barnett). New York: Scholastic Book Services, 1976.

Greenfield, Eloise. **Me & Neesie** (illustrated by Moneta Barnett). New York: Thomas Y. Crowell Company, 1975.

Haller, Danita Ross. **Not Just Any Ring** (illustrated by Deborah Kogan Ray). New York: Alfred A. Knopf, 1982 ($9.95, hardback).

With the help of her wise grandfather, Jesse learns that she must make her own magic and her own good days.

Hazen, Barbara Shook. **Tight Times** (illustrated by Trina Schart Hyman). New York: Penguin Books, 1979 ($3.50, paperback).

A young boy faces the daily realities of his family's economic struggles.

Head, Barry, and Jim Seguin. **Who Am I?** (photographs by Frank Dastolfo). Family Communications, Inc., 4802 Fifth Avenue, Pittsburgh, PA 15213, 1975.

Beautiful color photographs celebrate all the me's of a young girl—daughter, gardener, adventurer, student, friend. She also wears a hearing aid.

Highwater, Jamake. **Moonsong Lullaby** (illustrated by Marcia Keegan). New York: Lothrop, Lee & Shepard Books, 1981 ($11.25, hardback).

This lullaby fills us with images of the natural wonders of the night as American Indians once knew it.

Hill, Elizabeth Starr. **Evan's Corner** (illustrated by Nancy Grossman). New York: Holt, Rinehart and Winston, 1967.

In such a large family, Evan longs for a place of his own to fix up just as he wants it and to enjoy some peace and quiet.

Hines, Anna Grossnickle. **Daddy Makes the Best Spaghetti.** New York: Clarion Books, 1986 ($11.95, hardback).

Daddy has a way of turning everyday routines into delightful games.

Hughes, Shirley. **George the Babysitter.** Englewood Cliffs, NJ: Prentice-Hall, 1975 ($3.95, paperback).

The children help babysitter George make it through a busy day's activities.

Isadora, Rachel. **Ben's Trumpet.** New York: Greenwillow Books, 1979.

Set in the 1920's, this is the story of a young musician who feels the music and yearns to be part of it.

Isadora, Rachel. **City Seen from A to Z.** New York: Greenwillow Books, 1983 ($8.50, hardback).

Images of city life and the variety of its people fill this alphabet book.

Isadora, Rachel. **Max.** New York: Collier Books, 1976 ($3.95, paperback).

Max, star baseball player, discovers that ballet class is a great pre-game warmup on Saturday mornings.

Jensen, Virginia Allen. **Sara and the Door** (illustrated by Ann Strugnell). Reading, MA: Addison-Wesley Publishing Company, 1977.

Sara experiences the satisfaction that comes with solving a problem by herself.

Jonas, Ann. **The Quilt.** New York: Greenwillow Books, 1984 ($10.25, hardback).

A quilt made of scraps from her family's wardrobe keeps Sally awake.

Jonas, Ann. **The Trek.** New York: Greenwillow Books, 1985 ($11.75, hardback).

Two girls brave wild jungle adventures together on the way to school.

Keats, Ezra Jack. **Dreams.** New York: Collier Books, 1974.

Late one night Roberto sends his paper mouse on quite an adventure.

Keats, Ezra Jack. **Goggles!** New York: Collier Books, 1969.

Keats Ezra Jack. **Jennie's Hat.** New York: Harper & Row, Publishers, 1966.

Keats, Ezra Jack. **Louie.** New York: Scholastic Book Services, 1975.

Keats, Ezra Jack. **Pet Show!** New York: Collier Books, 1972.

Keats, Ezra Jack. **Peter's Chair.** New York: Harper & Row, Publishers, 1967.

Keats, Ezra Jack. **Regards to the Man in the Moon.** New York: Four Winds Press, 1981 ($12.95, hardback).

Keats, Ezra Jack. **Whistle for Willie.** New York: The Viking Press, 1964.

Klagsbrun, Francine (ed.). **Free to Be . . . You and Me.** New York: McGraw-Hill Book Company, 1974.

The stories and songs in both the record and book are delightful in their strong male and female characters. A storytelling, readaloud resource.

Lalli, Judy. **Feelings Alphabet.** B. L. Winch & Associates, 45 Hitching Post Drive, Building 2, Rolling Hills Estates, CA 90274, 1984 ($5.95, paperback).

An alphabet of emotions, which all people share, captured in photographs.

Little, Lessie Jones, and Eloise Greenfield. **I Can Do It By Myself** (illustrated by Carole Byard). New York: Thomas Y. Crowell Company, 1978.

Setting out by himself to buy a birthday gift for his mother gives Donald a special feeling of pride.

Mendoza, George. **Need A House? Call Ms. Mouse!** (illustrated by Doris Susan Smith). New York: Grosset & Dunlap, 1981 ($5.95, hardback).

Henrietta Mouse, world famous decorator, designs very special homes for her animal friends.

Munsch, Robert N. **The Paper Bag Princess** (illustrated by Michael Martchenko Toronto, Canada: Annick Press Ltd. (distributed by Firefly Books Ltd., 3520 Pharmacy Avenue, Unit 1-C, Scarborough, Ontario M1W 2T8), 1980.

In fairy tale style Munsch creates a princess who sets out to rescue a prince and then is not all that pleased with her prize.

Pogrebin, Letty Cottin (ed.). **Stories for Free Children.** New York: McGraw-Hil 1982 ($9.95, paperback).

A collection of stories which reflect diversity and cross barriers. A readaloud or storytelling resource.

Pomerantz, Charlotte. **The Tamarindo Puppy and Other Poems** (illustrated by Byron Barton). New York: Greenwillow Books, 1980.

Poems with English and Spanish words and lines mixed together.

Quinsey, Mary Beth. **Why Does That Man Have Such a Big Nose?** (photograph by Wilson Chan). Parenting Press, Inc., 7744 31st Avenue. NE, Seattle, Washington 98115, 1986 ($4.95, paperback).

Questions children often ask about physical differences are answered straightforwardly. Also a good reference for teachers.

Scott, Ann Herbert. **Sam** (illustrated by Symeon Shimin). New York: McGraw-Hill Book Company, 1967 ($11.95, hardback).

When Sam just can't take being left out anymore his family responds with a job that's just perfect for him.

Schweitzer, Byrd Baylor. **Amigo** (illustrated by Garth Williams). New York: Collier Books, 1963 ($2.95, paperback).

Francisco, a boy, and Amigo, a prairie dog, both long to have a pet—so they team up!

Schweitzer, Byrd Baylor. **One Small Blue Bead.** New York: The Macmillan Company, 1965.

The discovery of a blue bead takes us back to ancient times and a small boy who aids an old man's search for other men.

Scott, Ann Herbert. **On Mother's Lap** (illustrated by Glo Coalson). New York: McGraw-Hill Book Company, 1972 ($10.95, hardback).

Michael learns there's always room on mother's lap, even for a baby sister. Illustrations depict Eskimo life.

Spier, Peter. **People.** New York: Doubleday & Co., Inc., 1980 ($11.95, hardback).

A beautiful book that discusses and celebrates the scope of human diversity—appearance, wealth, ability, preferences, religion—and the commonalties which bind us together.

Steptoe, John. **Daddy Is a Monster . . . Sometimes.** New York: Harper & Row Junior Books Group, 1980 ($4.95, paperback).

His children can turn this daddy into a monster when they push him too far.

Waber, Bernard. **Ira Sleeps Over.** Boston, MA: Houghton Mifflin Co., 1972.

Ira has a difficult time deciding whether or not to take his teddy bear along on his overnight at Reggie's house.

Waterton, Betty. **A Salmon for Simon** (illustrated by Ann Blades). Vancouver, BC: Douglas & McIntyre (distributed by Salem House Ltd., 462 Boston Street, Topsfield, MA 01983), 1978 ($3.95, paperback).

Simon spends his summer fishing for a salmon. Then, just when he gives up, he catches one in a most unusual way.

Welber, Robert. **The Train** (illustrated by Deborah Ray). New York: Pantheon Books, 1972.

Out of print—but if you can find it, one of the few books depicting a biracial family. Story of a young girl whose love of trains eventually overcomes her fears of the journey to watch them.

Williams, Barbara. **Kevin's Grandma** (illustrated by Kay Chorao). New York: Scholastic Book Services, 1975.

Kevin tells stories of adventures with his grandma that would make anyone envious—but could he be exaggerating?

Williams, Vera B. **A Chair for My Mother.** New York: Greenwillow Books, 1982 ($3.95, paperback).

Fire destroyed their possessions so a girl and her mother and grandmother work together to save for an overstuffed chair in which to relax and snuggle.

Williams, Vera B. **Cherries and Cherry Pits.** New York: Greenwillow Books, 1986 ($11.75, hardback).

Through her drawings and stories, Bidemmi creates a very special and unusual way of drawing humankind together.

Williams, Vera B. **Something Special for Me.** New York: Mulberry Books, 1983.

Yarbrough, Camille. **Cornrows** (illustrated by Carole Byard). New York: Coward-McCann, 1979 ($3.95, paperback).

As Mama and Great-Grammaw braid their children's hair, stories are woven, too, about meanings behind the patterns in celebration of the black tradition.

Yashima, Taro. **Umbrella.** New York: The Viking Press, 1958.

When Momo gets a new umbrella, it's very hard to wait for rain—and then, such joy.

Special Relationships

Barrett, Judi. **Cloudy With a Chance of Meatballs** (illustrated by Ron Barrett). New York: Atheneum, 1978.

Grandpa has a lively imagination that almost brings his tall tale to life.

Caines, Jeannette. **Daddy** (illustrated by Ronald Himler). New York: Harper & Row, Publishers, 1977.

Weekend visits with her father are full of comfortable playfulness and dependable delight for Windy.

Caines, Jeannette. **Just Us Women** (illustrated by Pat Cummings). New York: Harper & Row, Publishers, 1982 ($3.95, paperback).

Caines, Jeannette. **Window Wishing** (illustrated by Kevin Brooks). New York: Harper & Row, Publishers, 1980.

Flournoy, Valerie. **The Patchwork Quilt** (illustrated by Jerry Pinkney). New York: Dial Books for Young Readers, 1985 ($10.95, hardback).

Creating a quilt helps Tanya and her grandmother weave the past and present together to tell the story of their family.

Fox, Mem. **Wilfrid Gordon McDonald Partridge** (illustrated by Julie Vivas). New York: Kane/Miller Book Publishers, 1985. ($9.95, hardback).

This is my favorite book about friendship across generations—a charming story of how a young boy helps his older friend find her memories.

Hest, Amy. **The Crack-of-Dawn Walkers** (illustrated by Amy Schwartz). New York: Macmillan Publishing Company, 1984 ($9.95, hardback).

A Sunday morning walk with her grandfather is a very special time for Sadie.

Keats, Ezra Jack. **Apt. 3.** New York: The Macmillan Company, 1971.
Curiosity about a neighbor and his music lead Sam and Ben to a new friend.

Mahy, Margaret. **Ultra-Violet Catastrophe!** (illustrated by Brian Froud). New York: Parents' Magazine Press, 1975.
Sally and Great-Uncle Magnus are two of a kind and their friendship develops during a walk together.

Miles, Miska. **Annie and the Old One** (illustrated by Peter Parnall). Boston, MA: Little, Brown and Company, 1971 ($11.95, hardback).
Annie's love for the Old One makes it difficult for her to let go, but eventually she comes to understand that aging and dying are a natural part of living.

Steptoe, John. **Stevie.** New York: Harper & Row, Publishers, 1969.
Sometimes a younger child—even a playmate—can seem like a nuisance until he moves away.

Viorst, Judith. **Rosie and Michael** (illustrated by Lorna Tomei). New York: Atheneum, 1974.
Best friends, Rosie and Michael, enjoy and understand each other, for better or for worse.

Wittman, Sally. **A Special Trade** (illustrated by Karen Gundersheimer). New York: Harper & Row, Publishers, 1978.
Nelly and Bartholomew are neighbors of very different ages, special friends who take turns caring for each other.

Books for Infants and Toddlers Reflecting Diversity

Ahlberg, Janet and Allan. **The Baby's Catalogue.** Boston, MA: Little, Brown and Company, 1982 ($11.95, hardback).

Bang, Molly. **Ten, Nine, Eight.** New York: Greenwillow Books, 1983.

Crews, Donald. **Bicycle Race.** New York: Greenwillow Books, 1985 ($11.75, hardback).

Hughes, Shirley. **When We Went to the Park.** New York: Lothrop, Lee & Shepard Books, 1985 ($4.95, hardback).

Jonas, Ann. **When You Were a Baby.** New York: Greenwillow Books, 1982.

Keats, Ezra Jack. **The Snowy Day.** New York: The Viking Press, 1962.

O'Brien, Anne Sibley. **Come Play with Us.** New York: Holt, Rinehart and Winston, 1985 ($3.95, hardback).

O'Brien, Anne Sibley. **I'm Not Tired.** New York: Holt, Rinehart and Winston, 1985 ($3.95, hardback).

Ormerod, Jan. **Dad's Back.** New York: Lothrop, Lee & Shepard Books, 1985 ($4.95, hardback). Also **Messy Baby, Reading, Sleeping, and Young Joe.**

Life in Other Places

• **Africa**

Feelings, Muriel. **Jamboo Means Hello: Swahili Alphabet Book** (illustrated by Tom Feelings). New York: Dial Books for Young Readers, 1974.

Feelings, Muriel. **Moja Means One** (illustrated by Tom Feelings). New York: The Dial Press, 1971.

Graham, Lorenz. **Song of the Boat** (illustrated by Leo and Diane Dillon). New York: Thomas Y. Crowell Company, 1975.

• **The Caribbean**

Lessac, Frane. **My Little Island.** New York: J. B. Lippincott, 1985 ($11.50, hardback).

• **India**

Bonnici, Peter. **The Festival** (illustrated by Lisa Kopper). Carolrhoda Books, 241 First Avenue North, Minneapolis, MN 55401 ($8.95, hardback), 1985. Also **The First Rains.**

• **South Africa**

Lewin, Hugh. **Jafta** (illustrated by Lisa Kopper). Minneapolis, MN: Carolrhoda Books, 1983. Also **Jafta and the Wedding, Jafta—The Journey, Jafta—The Town, Jafta's Father,** and **Jafta's Mother**

• **Around the World**

Abells, Chana Byers. **The Children We Remember.** New York: Greenwillow Books, 1983 ($9.95, hardback).

A moving account of the Holocaust told through photographs of its children.

Anno, Mitsumasa, et al. **All in a Day.** New York: Philomel Books, 1986 ($13.95, hardback).

Nine celebrated artists have brought the world's children together in this work of friendship and peace. Activities, time, and season in 8 different countries are illustrated over a 24 hour period, accentuating ways we are all alike.

Feeney, Stephanie. **A is for Aloha** (photographs by Hella Hammid). Honolulu, HI: The University Press of Hawaii, 1980.

A beautiful alphabet book in black and white photographs of Hawaiian life.

Goldfarb, Mace, M. D. **Fighters, Refugees, Immigrants: A Story of the Hmong.** Minneapolis, MN: Carolrhoda Books, 1982 ($9.95, hardback).

Although the text is written for older children, the color photographs of life in a refugee camp in Thailand are an important resource.

Raynor, Dorka. **Grandparents Around the World.** Chicago, IL: Albert Whitman & Company, 1977.

Raynor, Dorka. **My Friends Live in Many Places.** Chicago, IL: Albert Whitman & Company, 1980.

Rylant, Cynthia. **When I Was Young in the Mountains** (illustrated by Diane Goode). New York: E. P. Dutton, 1982 ($9.95, hardback).

Beautiful images of a childhood in Appalachia.

Smith, MaryLou M. **Grandmother's Adobe Dollhouse** (illustrated by Ann Blackstone). New Mexico Magazine, Bataan Memorial Building, Santa Fe, NM 87503, 1984 ($15.00, hardback).

Not exactly another place, but this book shares information about Pueblo Indians and the culture of New Mexico.

Svend, Otto S. (translated by Joan Tate). **Children of the Yangtze River.** London: Pelham Books Ltd. (distributed by Merrimack Publishers' Circle, 47 Pelham Road, Salem, NH 03079), 1985 ($8.95, hardback).

Trinca, Rod, and Kerry Argent. **One Wooly Wombat** (illustrated by Kerry Argent). New York: Kane/Miller Book Publishers, 1982 ($8.95, hardback).

A delightful counting book with Australian flavor.

Books About Diversity

• Biracial

Adoff, Arnold. **Black is Brown is Tan** (illustrated by Emily McCully). New York: Harper & Row, Publishers, 1973.

A story-poem about a house full of love and adults and children of many colors.

Rosenberg, Maxine B. **Living in Two Worlds** (photographs by George Ancona). New York: Lothrop, Lee & Shepard Books, 1986 ($10.25, hardback).

Biracial children share their feelings about themselves and their heritage and the prejudices they encounter. Wonderful photographs—a great variety of ethnic and racial mixtures.

• Family Composition

Bauer, Caroline Feller. **My Mom Travels A Lot** (illustrated by Nancy Winslow Parker). New York: Frederick Warne, 1981 ($4.95, paperback).

Perry, Patricia, and Marietta Lynch. **Mommy and Daddy Are Divorced.** New York: Dial Books for Young Readers, 1985 ($3.95, paperback).

Rosenberg, Maxine B. **Being a Twin, Having a Twin** (photographs by George Ancona). New York: Lothrop, Lee & Shepard Books, 1985 ($10.25, hardback).

Simon, Norma. **All Kinds of Families** (illustrated by Joe Lasker). Chicago, IL: Albert Whitman & Company, 1976.

• Disabilities

Brown, Tricia. **Some Special, Just Like You** (photographs by Fran Ortiz). New York: Holt, Rinehart and Winston, 1982 ($11.95, hardback).

Cairo, Shelley. **Our Brother Has Down's Syndrome** (photographs by Irene McNeil). Toronto, Canada: Annick Press (distributed by Firefly Books, 3520 Pharmacy Avenue, Unit 1-C, Scarborough, Ontario, Canada M1W 2T8), 1985

Chapman, Elizabeth. **Suzy** (illustrated by Margery Gill). The Bodley Head Ltd., 9 Bow Street, London, England WC2E 7AL, 1982 ($6.95, hardback).

Corrigan, Kathy. **Emily Umily** (illustrated by Vlasta van Kampen). Toronto, Canada: Annick Press Ltd., 1984.

Peterson, Jeanne Whitehouse. **I Have a Sister—My Sister is Deaf** (illustrated by Deborah Ray). New York: Harper & Row, Publishers, 1977.

• Sex Roles

Kempler, Susan, Doreen Rappaport, Michele Spirn. **A Man Can Be . . .** (photographs by Russel Dian). Human Sciences Press, 72 Fifth Avenue, New York, NY 10017, 1981.

Merriam, Eve. **Boys & Girls, Girls & Boys** (illustrated by Harriet Sherman). New York: Holt, Rinehart and Winston, 1972.

Portnoy, Mindy Avra. **Ima on the Bima** (illustrated by Steffi Karen Rubin). Kar-Ben Copies, Inc., 6800 Tildenwood Lane, Rockville, MD 20852, 1986 ($4.95, paperback; $10.95, hardback).

Tales and Legends

Don't forget the wealth of beautiful and interesting legends from around the world.

Within Your Reach—
Resources on Diversity

Beginning Equal Project. **Beginning Equal: A Manual About Nonsexist Childrearing for Infants and Toddlers.** New York: Women's Action Alliance and Pre-School Association, 1983.

A series of workshop materials designed to help caregivers and/or parents explore gender issues as they impact on very young children. These workshops grew out of the research project with the same name; topics include exploring your own sex-role attitudes, adult-child inter-actions, identifying conflicts and developing strategies for change, and analyzing toys and materials. Alternative workshop formats included. Workshop materials also in Spanish.

Bernstein, Bonnie, and Leigh Blair. **North American Crafts Workshop.** Belmont, CA: David S. Lake Publishers, 1982.

Craft ideas to use with young children.

Boston Women's Health Book Collective. **Ourselves and Our Children.** New York: Random House, 1978.

Exploring families and parenting—the diversity, issues, richness.

Caston, Don. **Easy-to-Make Aids for Your Handicapped Child: A Guide for Parents and Teachers.** Englewood Cliffs, NJ: Prentice-Hall, 1981.

How-to plans for building and customizing aids for children with special needs such as back rests, toilets, climbing frames, walkers.

Cole, Ann, Carolyn Haas, Elizabeth Heller, Betty Weinberger. **Children Are Children Are Children** (illustrated by Lois Axeman). Boston, MA: Little, Brown and Company, 1978.

Activity ideas based on cultures of Brazil, France, Iran, Japan, Nigeria, and USSR.

Deiner, Penny Low. **Resources for Teaching Young Children with Special Needs.** New York: Harcourt Brace Jovanovich, 1983.

A resource book based on the premise that all children sometimes have special needs. Focuses on areas of need and provides ideas for curriculum adaptations and then offers activities designed to help meet needs. Looks at cultural and intellectual as well as physical needs.

Edwards, Carolyn Pope (with Patricia G. Ramsey). **Promoting Social and Moral Development in Young Children.** New York: Teachers College Press, 1986.

An examination of the social cognitive growth of children ages two through six, based on a Piagetian understanding of how children construct knowledge of themselves and their world. Includes sections on sex roles and cultural categories—along with ideas for conducting thinking games with young children on these topics. Well written with anecdotes.

Ehrlich, Virginia Z. **Gifted Children: A Guide for Parents and Teachers.** New York: Trillium Press, 1985.

Written for both teachers and parents, this discussion of giftedness includes criteria for identification, special needs, educational needs, and careers.

Fluegelman, Andrew (ed.). **The New Games Book.** New York: Doubleday & Company, 1976.

Non-competitive games for all ages.

Froschl, Merle, Linda Colon, Ellen Rubin, and Barbara Sprung. **Including All of Us: An Early Childhood Curriculum About Disability.** Educational Equity Concepts, 440 Park Avenue South, New York, NY 10016 (Distributed by Gryphon House, PO Box 275, Mt. Rainier, MD 20712), 1984.

*An inclusive curriculum designed to be nonsexist and multicultural and to increase understanding of disabilities. The three curriculum units presented—Same/Different, Body Parts, and Transportation—include activities, materials suggestions, and well-conceived rationale and guidelines. Each integrates the **New Friends** dolls (see listing on page 153). Excellent curriculum model with extensive resource listing.*

Gomez, Gloria. **An Introductory Guide to Bilingual-Bicultural/ Multicultural Education: Beyond Tacos, Eggrolls and Grits.** Dubuque, IA: Kendall/Hunt Publishing Company, 1982.

A guide designed to help programs and individuals examine philosophies and approaches to multicultural education. Questions to promote thought and discussion and self-assessment tools.

Haegert, Dorothy. **Children of the First People.** Tillacum Library, 202-986 Homer Street, Vancouver, BC, Canada V6B 2W7, 1983.

Beautiful photographs of Native Canadian Indians portray contemporary culture. Accompanying narratives by Native Elders recall the past. Not designed for young children—but photographs make it a valuable resource.

Heekin, Shelley, and Patricia Mengel (eds.). **New Friends.** Chapel Hill Training-Outreach Project, Lincoln Center, Merritt Mill Road, Chapel Hill, NC 27514.

A preschool-kindergarten curriculum designed to help teachers provide accurate information about disabilities to young children and families of children with special needs through the use of teacher-made dolls. Teacher's Manual includes instructions for doll construction, suggestions for leading discussions on specific disabilities, ideas for related classroom activities, and guidelines for answering children's questions and exploring feelings and attitudes. Trainer's Notebook for conducting workshops on the New Friends program and an introductory slide / tape presentation are also available.

Hungry Wolf, Adolf and Beverly. **Children of the Sun.** New York: William Morrow and Company, 1987.

Resource for images of Indian family life as it once was.

Kendall, Frances E. **Diversity in the Classroom.** New York: Teachers College Press, 1983.

Multicultural education comes about through a thorough understanding of child development, examination of our own attitudes, the support of parents, and careful preparation of the environment and the curriculum. Guidelines given for developing a curriculum unit based on diversity. Extensive bibliography.

Lee, Rhonda (ed.). **Guide to Nonsexist Language and Visuals.** University of Wisconsin-Extension, 432 North Lake Street, Madison,

WI 53706, 1985. (Individual copies [1-19] $2 each postpaid; bulk orders [20+] $1.50. Order individual copies from UW-Extension Bookstore, bulk orders from Sheila Mulcahy, both at address above.)

A helpful guide for replacing sexist references with liberating terms.

McNeill, Earldene, Velma Schmidt, Judy Allen. **Cultural Awareness for Young Children.** Dallas, TX: The Learning Tree (distributed by Gryphon House, PO Box 275, Mt. Rainier, MD 20712), 1981.

Curriculum ideas for Asian, Black, Cowboy, Eskimo, Mexican, and Native American cultures. Excellent resource.

Meltzer, Milton (ed.). **The Black Americans: A History in Their Own Words.** New York: Thomas Y. Crowell, 1964.

A resource for self-enlightenment and background information for classroom discussion and storytelling, the history of Black Americans is told through pieces of their own writings—dramatic and real.

Multicultural Project for Communication and Education. **Caring for Children in a Social Context: Eliminating Racism, Sexism and Other Patterns of Discrimination.** The Multicultural Project for Communication and Education, 678 Massachusetts Avenue, PO Box 125, Cambridge, MA 02139.

A thoughtful discussion of patterns of discrimination with specific suggestions for liberating your program or your classroom. Excellent resource for examining where you are and planning what you want to become.

Orlick, Terry. **The Cooperative Sports & Games Book.** New York: Pantheon Books, 1978.

Ideas for cooperative play, adaptable to a variety of ages and needs.

Paley, Vivian Gussin. **White Teacher.** Cambridge, MA: Harvard University Press, 1979.

This is a story of self-discovery told through the experiences of a White kindergarten teacher and her group of children, Black and White. She moves from being unable to talk about differences to become an adult guide, comfortably answering and asking questions, helping children to understand themselves and each other—acquiring social and intellectual skills necessary for improving life.

Pogrebin, Letty Cottin. **Growing Up Free: Raising Your Child in the 80's.** New York: McGraw-Hill Book Company, 1980.

An in-depth consideration of the impact of sex roles and sexism as they mold the lives of children. A strong statement with practical suggestions for working to help children reach their full potential.

Ramsey, Patricia G. **Teaching and Learning in a Diverse World.** New York: Teachers College Press, 1987.

A multicultural perspective can be built into all programs and all aspects of the curriculum. Early childhood educators have a rich opportunity for creating new and liberated understanding in young children. Extensive practical suggestions.

Rappaport, Lisa. **Recipes for Fun: Play Activities and Games for Young Children With Disabilities and Their Families** (illustrated by Ingrid Gehle). Let's Play to Grow, 1350 New York Avenue NW, Suite 500, Washington, DC 20005, 1986.

Part of the Let's Play to Grow program for families of children with disabilities, this resource is filled with ideas for games and play activities which children and adults can enjoy as they explore the world together. Adaptations for specific impairments included.

Saracho, Olivia N., and Bernard Spodek (eds.). **Understanding the Multicultural Experience in Early Childhood Education.** Washington, DC: NAEYC, 1983.

A scholarly collection of varied concerns about the impact and implications of early childhood education for different cultural groups.

Schmidt, Velma E., and Earldene McNeill. **Cultural Awareness: A Resource Bibliography.** Washington, DC: NAEYC, 1978.

Extensive annotated bibliography of resources, listed by cultural group. Includes books for children; materials and experiential resources; and books, articles, and catalogs for adults.

Schuman, Jo Miles. **Art From Many Hands: Multicultural Art Projects.** Worcester, MA: Davis Publications, 1981.

Authentic arts and crafts from many cultures. Not targeted to young children; excellent teacher resource for inspiration and background.

Shannon-Thornberry, Milo. **The Alternate Celebrations Catalogue.** New York: The Pilgrim Press, 1982.

Discussion of the messages inherent in our ways of celebrating and in our choices of things to celebrate. Suggestions for more meaningful celebrations.

Smith, Jamie C. **Beginning Early: Adult Responsibilities to Gifted Young Children.** New York: Trillium Press, 1986.

A comprehensive list (checklist format) of the responsibilities involved for administrators, teachers, parents, and programs in nurturing the growth of gifted children.

Souweine, Judith, Sheila Crimmins, and Carolyn Mazel. **Mainstreaming: Ideas for Teaching Young Children.** Washington, DC: NAEYC, 1981.

Approaches and strategies for integrating children with special needs into the early childhood classroom—developing an individualized educational plan, designing the environment, and planning the curriculum.

Sprung, Barbara (ed.). **Perspectives on Non-Sexist Early Childhood Education.** New York: Teachers College Press, 1978.

A collection of thought-provoking articles related to issues of sexism in early childhood. Some pieces discuss research, while others examine theory and practice.

Texas Department of Human Resources. **Culture and Children.** Texas Department of Human Resources, Child Development Division, PO Box 2960, Austin, TX 78769, August 1984.

Ideas for classroom activities and suggestions for resources—based on cultural groups in Texas.

van Straalen, Alice. **The Book of Holidays Around the World.** New York: E. P. Dutton, 1986.

A holiday for every day of the year (variable date explanations keep it timeless). A beautiful resource for people who like to celebrate.

Williams, Leslie R., and Yvonne De Gaetano. **Alerta.** Menlo Park, CA: Addison-Wesley Publishing Company, 1985.

An excellent guide for developing a multicultural bilingual program based on the experiences and observations of the children within the program. Content grows from the children in the context of their

*cultures and communities and permeates all areas of learning and
activity. Valuable planning guide.*

Wenning, Jessie, and Sheli Wortis. **Made By Human Hands: A
Curriculum for Teaching Young Children About Work and
Working People**. The Multicultural Project for Communication and
Education, Inc., 71 Cherry Street, Cambridge, MA 02139, (617) 492-1063.

*A well-conceived curriculum about work which reflects diversity and
contemporary realities. Begins with the work of both adults and
children within the center, then moves out into the family and
community.*

Newsletters and Organizations

Communique, The Interracial Family Alliance, PO Box 16248, Houston,
TX 77222. (Quarterly—$10 per year). This national organization will
provide you with addresses for local interracial family organizations.

Council on Interracial Books Bulletin, 1841 Broadway, New York, NY
10023. (8 issues per year—$12 individual, $18 institution)

Equal Play, Women's Action Alliance, 370 Lexington Avenue, New
York, NY 10017, (212) 532-8330. (Twice a year—$12.50 individual
subscription, $20 institutional subscription. Single copies $7.50)

Faces: The Magazine About People, Cobblestone Publishing, 20 Grove
Street, Peterborough, NH 03458, (603) 924-7209. (10 issues per
year—$16.50, Canada and other foreign countries $4 additional per
year. Single copies $1.95)

Gifted Children Monthly, Gifted and Talented Publications, 213
Hollydell Drive, Sewell, NJ 08080, (609) 582-0277. (11 issues per
year—$24 one year, $44 two years, $64 three years; Canada and other
foreign countries add $5 per year)

Multicultural Project for Communication and Education **Newsletter**, 71
Cherry Street, Cambridge, MA 02139, (617) 492-1063. (Per year: Friend
(Individual) $10, Friend (Institution) $25, Patron $40-64, Sponsor $65-99,
Benefactor $100 and over)

News Digest, National Information Center for Handicapped Children
and Youth, Box 1492, Washington, DC 20013. (Free)

The Council for Exceptional Children, 1920 Association Drive, Reston,
VA 22091-1589, (703) 620-3660.

U.S. Committee for UNICEF, 331 East 38th Street, New York, NY 1001 (212) 686-5522.

Equipment, Toys, and Materials

ARTS Inc., 32 Market Street, New York, NY 10002, (212) 962-8231. Chinese and Hispanic music, activities and games—booklets and cassettes. Also an interesting tape of ethnic lullabies from New York City.

Bestfriends, PO Box 315, Winter Park, CO 80482, (303) 726-8388. Soft sculpture dolls depicting children with disabilities. Can be custom made.

Caedmon, 1995 Broadway, New York, NY 10023, (800) 223-0420. Records and cassettes.

Children's Book & Music Center, PO Box 1130, Santa Monica, CA 9040 1130, (800) 443-1856 (in California, (213) 829-0215). Books and records for children, some teacher resources.

Choice Puzzles—Non-Sexist Puzzles for Children, PO Box 22609, Seattle, WA 98122, (206) 325-4882 (Lyle Rudensey). Quality puzzles handcrafted from color photographs of women (carpenter, electrician, welder, bicycle racers) and men (folkdancer, hairdresser, early childhood teacher, and quiltmaker). $12 each, plus 15% shipping—$10 each for orders of 5 or more. Will also make puzzle from your color slide.

Claudia's Caravan, PO Box 1582, Alameda, CA, (415) 521-7871. An extensive collection of multilingual, multicultural materials.

Community Playthings and **Rifton Equipment for the Handicapped** Route 213, Rifton, NY 12471, (914) 658-3141 or (914) 658-3143. Catalog of quality equipment for children with disabilities and general catalog.

Crafts and Creative Alternatives, Pueblo to People, 1616 Montrose, Houston, TX 77006, (713) 523-1197. Handcrafted items from Central America. Note textiles.

Creative Concepts For Children, 3743 East Glenrosa, Phoenix, AZ 8501 (602) 954-8177. Nonsexist, multicultural puppets. Also made to order and personalized.

Daystar Designs, PO Box 12892, Dept. KT, Salem, OR 97309, (503) 390-0346. Patterns to sew. Authentic Korean hanbok for doll ($5), children ($6), adults ($7).

Early Learning Experiences, Asper Folta Consultants, PO Box 729, Haines, AK 99827, (907) 766-2580. Curriculum materials reflecting Alaskan cultures.

Educational Records, 472 East Paces Ferry Road, Atlanta, GA 30305. Records.

The Fibar System, Robert Godfrey Ltd., 823 West Street, Harrison, NY 10528, (800) FIBAR-A1 (in New York, (914) 835-1511). New playground surface makes play area accessible for children using wheelchairs, crutches, or walkers. Sounds good—check it out.

Folkway Records, 632 Broadway, New York, NY 10012, (212) 982-1840. Records.

Gryphon House, PO Box 275, Mt. Rainier, MD 20712, (800) 638-0928 (in Maryland, (301) 779-6200). Excellent collection of books for children and teacher resources.

Hal's Pals, For Challenged Kids by Mattel, Inc., 5150 Rosecrans Avenue, Hawthorne, CA 90250, (800) 227-3800. Dolls with physical disabilities and their own special equipment (only Black and White races available).

Holt International Children's Services, PO Box 2880, Eugene, OR 97402, (503) 687-2202 (Kathy Blacketter). Dolls, books, purses, and clothing from India.

Howe Press, Perkins School for the Blind, 175 North Beacon Street, Watertown, MA 02172, (617) 924-3434. Books in both print and Braille.

Huggy Bean, Golden Ribbon Playthings Inc., 575 Madison Avenue, Suite 1006, New York, NY 10022, (212) 605-0122. Charming Black character doll. Extended family and Hispanic friend dolls also available.

Kapable Kids, PO Box 3912, New Hyde Park, NY 11040, (516) 437-2882. Materials and equipment designed to meet needs of children with disabilities.

Kar-Ben Copies, Inc., 6800 Tildenwood Lane, Rockville, MD 20852, (301) 984-8733. Books reflecting the Jewish tradition.

Lauri puzzle, "Familiar People," available through many early childhood materials catalogues. Represents the variety in human life. Excellent.

Music for Little People, Star Route, Redway, CA 95560, (800) 443-9990 (in California and Alaska, (707) 923-2040). Cassette tapes and interesting musical instruments.

Pacific Cascade Records, 47534 McKenzie Highway, Vida, OR 97488-9707, (503) 896-3290. Records and cassette tapes.

Save the Children's Craft Shop, PO Box 3373, Wallingford, CT 06494, (800) 225-7694 (in Connecticut, (203) 235-4025). Items from around the world. Note instruments.

U.S. Committee for UNICEF, 331 East 38th Street, New York, NY 1001((212) 686-5522. Materials with global focus. Ask for **Publications and Educational Materials Catalog**.

Weston Woods, Weston, CT 06883-9989, (800) 243-5020 (in Connecticut, (203) 226-3355). Book and record/cassette tape sets of many titles from children's booklist. Also note videocassettes of: *Why Mosquitoes Buzz in People's Ears, Alexander and the Car with a Missing Headlight, The Five Chinese Brothers, Tikki Tikki Tembo, The Story About Ping, Where Stories Come From.*

(Some of the resources listed in this listing were recommended by authors of articles in the book.)